The Four Tendencies

ALSO BY GRETCHEN RUBIN

Better Than Before
Happier at Home
The Happiness Project
Forty Ways to Look at JFK
Power Money Fame Sex: A User's Guide
Profane Waste (with Dana Hoey)

The Four Tendencies

THE INDISPENSABLE PERSONALITY PROFILES THAT REVEAL HOW TO MAKE YOUR LIFE BETTER (AND OTHER PEOPLE'S LIVES BETTER, TOO)

GRETCHEN RUBIN

www.tworoadsbooks.com

First published in Great Britain in 2017 by Two Roads
An imprint of John Murray Press
An Hachette UK company

A CIP catalogue record for this title is available from the British Library

Trade Paperback ISBN 978 1 473 66285 8
Ebook ISBN 978 1 473 66286 5
Audio Digital Download 978 1 473 66566 8

Printed and bound by Clays Ltd, St Ives plc

Hodder & Stoughton policy is to use papers that are natural, renewable
and recyclable products and made from wood grown in sustainable
forests. The logging and manufacturing processes are expected to
conform to the environmental regulations of the country of origin.

Hodder & Stoughton Ltd
Carmelite House
50 Victoria Embankment
London EC4Y 0DZ

www.hodder.co.uk

For Christy Fletcher (Questioner)

CONTENTS

Your Tendency

Upholder

"Discipline is my freedom"

Questioner

"I'll comply—if you convince me why"

Obliger

"You can count on me, and I'm counting on you to count on me"

Rebel

"You can't make me, and neither can I"

9: Understanding the Rebel

"It's so hard when I have to, and so easy when I want to"

Strengths • Weaknesses • Variations Within the Tendency • How Others Can Influence Rebels to Meet an Expectation • How Rebels Can Influence Themselves to Meet an Expectation • Why Rebels May Be Drawn to Lives of High Regulation

10: Dealing with a Rebel

"You're not the boss of me"

Work • Spouse • Child • Health Client • Choosing a Career

Applying the Four Tendencies

Appendix

Finally I am coming to the conclusion that my highest ambition is to be what I already am.

—*Journal of Thomas Merton* (Rebel)

YOUR TENDENCY

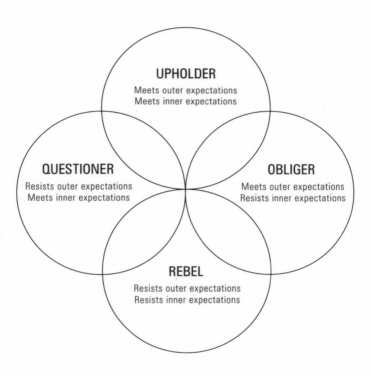

UPHOLDER
Meets outer expectations
Meets inner expectations

QUESTIONER
Resists outer expectations
Meets inner expectations

OBLIGER
Meets outer expectations
Resists inner expectations

REBEL
Resists outer expectations
Resists inner expectations

1

The Four Tendencies

I didn't realize it at the time, but when I walked through the door of the Atlantic Grill restaurant one blustery winter afternoon, I was heading to one of the most significant conversations of my life.

As I bit into my cheeseburger and my friend picked at her salad, she made a comment that would occupy my mind for years. In an offhand way, she mentioned, "I want to get myself in the habit of running, but I can't, and it really bothers me." Then she added, in a crucial observation, "When I was on the high school track team, I never missed track practice, so why can't I go running now?"

"Why?" I echoed.

"Well, you know, it's so hard to make time for ourselves."

"Hmmm," I said.

We started talking about other things, but even after we'd said good-bye, I couldn't stop thinking about our exchange. She was the same person she'd been in high school, and she was aiming to do the same activity. She'd been able to go running in the past, but not now. Why? Was it her age, her motivation, her family situation, the location, team spirit, or something else?

She assumed that we all have trouble "making time for ourselves." But actually I *don't* have any trouble making time for myself. How were she and I different from each other?

I would spend the next few years trying to answer these questions.

The Origin of the Four Tendencies

They say there are two kinds of people in the world: those who divide the world into two kinds of people, and those who don't.

I'm definitely the first kind. My great interest is human nature, and I constantly search for patterns to identify what we do and why we do it.

I've spent years studying happiness and habits, and it has become obvious to me that there's no magic, one-size-fits-all answer for building a happier, healthier, more productive life. Different strategies work for different people—in fact, what works for one person may be the *very opposite* of what works for someone else. Some people are morning people; some are night people. Some do better when they abstain from a strong temptation; others, when they indulge in moderation. Some people love simplicity; some thrive in abundance.

And not only that. As I pondered my friend's observation about her running habit, I sensed that deep below the "night people vs. morning people" sorts of differences, there existed some kind of bedrock distinction that shaped people's natures—something profound, but also bold and obvious—that nevertheless eluded my vision.

To help figure out what I was missing, I posed a number of questions to readers of my website, including: "How do you feel about New Year's resolutions?" "Do you observe traffic regulations—why or why not?" "Would you ever sign up to take a class for fun?" As readers' responses poured in, I saw that distinct patterns were threaded through the various answers. It was almost *weird*—as though groups of people had agreed to answer from the same script.

For instance, about New Year's resolutions, a subset of people gave virtually identical answers: "I'll keep a resolution if it's useful, but I won't start on New Year's Day, because January 1 is an arbitrary date." They all used that word: "arbitrary." I was intrigued by this specific word choice, because the *arbitrariness* of the January 1 date had never bothered me. Yet these people were all giving the same answer—what did they have in common?

And many people answered, "I don't make New Year's resolutions anymore because I never manage to keep them—I never make time for myself."

Another group said, "I never make resolutions because I don't like to bind myself."

There was some meaningful design here, I knew it, but I just couldn't quite see it.

Then finally, after months of reflection, I had my eureka moment. As I sat at my desk in my home office, I happened to glance at my messy handwritten to-do list—and suddenly it hit me. The simple, decisive question was: *"How do you respond to expectations?"* I'd found it!

I'd discovered the key. I felt the same excitement that Archimedes must have felt when he stepped out of his bath.

I was sitting still, but my mind was racing forward with thoughts about *expectations*. I grasped at that moment that we all face two kinds of expectations:

- outer expectations—expectations others place on us, like meeting a work deadline

- inner expectations—expectations we place on ourselves, like keeping a New Year's resolution

And here was my crucial insight: Depending on a person's response to outer and inner expectations, that person falls into one of four distinct types:

Upholders respond readily to both outer expectations and inner expectations

Questioners question all expectations; they meet an expectation only if they believe it's justified, so in effect they respond only to inner expectations

Obligers respond readily to outer expectations but struggle to meet inner expectations

Rebels resist all expectations, outer and inner alike

It was that simple. With just one single, straightforward question, all of humanity sorted itself into these categories.

Now I understood why my friend had trouble forming the habit of running: She was an Obliger. When she'd had a team and a coach expecting her, she had no trouble showing up; when she faced her own inner expectations, she struggled. I understood those repetitious comments about New Year's resolutions. And I understood much, much more.

The Four Tendencies framework clarified the striking patterns of behavior I'd perceived, and I was able to make sense of what everyone else had seen—but no one else had noticed.

When I mapped the complete system on a sheet of paper, in four symmetrical overlapping circles, my framework showed the elegance of a fern frond or a nautilus shell. I truly felt that I'd uncovered a law of nature: human nature.

Or maybe I'd created something more like a Muggle Sorting Hat.

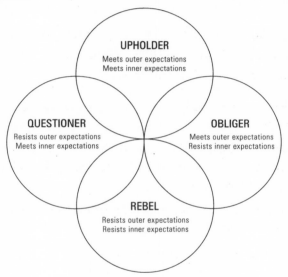

Once I'd identified the framework, I worked to deepen my understanding. "The Strategy of the Four Tendencies" became the first chapter in *Better Than Before,* my book about habit change; I wrote about the Four Tendencies on my website, gretchenrubin.com; my cohost and sister, Elizabeth Craft, and I talked about the Four Tendencies on our weekly podcast, *Happier with Gretchen Rubin.* Every time I discussed the framework, readers and listeners responded.

Most people can identify their Tendency from a brief

description, but for people who aren't sure or who want their answers to be analyzed, I designed a quiz. Hundreds of thousands of people have taken the Four Tendencies Quiz, which appears in chapter 2 or at happiercast.com/quiz. People's answers to the quiz, as well as their open-ended responses, gave me an additional trove of insights. (For one thing, I've noticed that people's Tendencies influence their willingness to take the quiz. Questioners sometimes ask, "Why should I spend my time and effort taking this quiz?" and Rebels sometimes think, "You're telling me to take this quiz? Well, I won't do it.")

To test my observations about the Four Tendencies, I decided to run a study of the framework among a nationally representative sample, to examine a geographically dispersed group of U.S. adults with a mix of gender, age, and household income.

The most important thing I discovered? The distribution of the Four Tendencies. At 41%, Obliger was the largest Tendency. Next came Questioner, at 24%. The Rebel Tendency had the fewest members, at 17%—I'm surprised that the survey put the number that high—and my own Tendency, the Upholder Tendency, was just slightly larger at 19%. The study also confirmed many of my observations about the Four Tendencies; for instance, when considering New Year's resolutions, Upholders are most likely to make them; Rebels dislike them; Questioners make resolutions when the time seems right rather than waiting for an arbitrary date; and often Obligers give up making resolutions altogether because they've struggled in the past.

As I refined the framework, I even assigned a color to each Tendency, by using the model of a traffic light. Yellow represents Questioners, because just as a yellow light cautions us to "wait" to decide whether to proceed, Questioners always ask "Wait, why?" before meeting an expectation. Green represents Obligers, who readily "go ahead." Red represents Rebels, who are most likely to "stop" or say no. Because there's no fourth traffic-light color, I chose blue for Upholders—which seems fitting.

The more I've studied the Tendencies, the more I've come to see their tremendous influence.

When we consider the Four Tendencies, we're better able to understand ourselves. This self-knowledge is crucial because we can build a happy life only on the foundation of our own nature, our own interests, and our own values.

Just as important, when we consider the Four Tendencies, we're better able to understand other people. We can live and work more effectively with others when we identify their Tendencies—as coworkers and bosses, teachers and coaches, husbands and wives, parents and children, health-care providers and patients.

Understanding the Four Tendencies gives us a richer understanding of the world.

How the Tendencies Weave Throughout Our Characters

Our Tendencies are hardwired: they're not the result of birth order, parenting style, religious upbringing, gender. They're not tied to extroversion or introversion. They don't change depending on whether we're at home, at work, with friends. And they don't change as we age. We bring these Tendencies into the world with us.

To a degree that surprises me, most people do indeed fall squarely into one of the four camps. While it can sometimes be difficult to identify a child's Tendency (I still can't figure out the Tendency of one of my daughters), by adulthood we clearly fit into a particular Tendency that shapes our perceptions and behavior in fundamental ways. Unless we go through some catastrophic, character-reshaping experience—such as a near-death experience, a grave illness, or a serious bout with addiction—our Tendencies don't change.

Depending on history and circumstance, though, our Tendency might be more or less helpful as we make our way in the world. In North Korea, a Questioner's questions might get him thrown in jail, while in Silicon Valley a Questioner's questions might win her a promotion.

Also, there's an enormous range of personalities, even among people who share the same Tendency. Regardless of Tendency, some people are more or less thoughtful than others, or ambitious, intellectual, controlling, charismatic, kind, anxious, energetic, or adventurous. These qualities dramatically influence how they express their Tendencies. An ambitious Rebel who wants to be a well-respected business leader will behave differently from one who doesn't care much about having a successful career.

People often argue that they're a mix of Tendencies. They tell me, "I'm an Obliger and an Upholder," or "My Tendency changes depending on where I am or who I'm with." This may sound sensible, but I must say that when I ask a few more questions, the person falls easily within a single Tendency, almost without exception.

To be sure, as discussed in the sections on "Variations Within the Tendency," people often "tip" in the direction of a Tendency that overlaps with their own, but nevertheless they still remain firmly located within a core Tendency.

And, of course, it's also true that no matter what our fundamental Tendency, a small part of each of us is Upholder, Questioner, Obliger, and Rebel.

All of us meet an expectation when we don't want to bear the consequences of ignoring it. The Rebel wears his seat belt after he pays a few big fines.

All of us may question why we should have to meet an expectation, or become annoyed by inefficiency, or refuse to do something that seems arbitrary.

We all meet some expectations because they're important to someone else. The most determined Upholder will sacrifice her regular Monday-morning meeting if her child is recovering from surgery.

And whatever our Tendency, we share a desire for autonomy. We prefer to be asked rather than ordered to do something, and if our feeling of being controlled by others becomes too strong, it can trigger "reactance," a resistance to something that's experienced as a threat to our freedom or our ability to choose.

After I'd described the Four Tendencies at a conference, a guy walked up to me and said, "I think everyone should be able to drive at whatever speed they think is safe, so I must be a Questioner!"

I smiled, but the fact is, it's not a simple matter of "I ignore the speed limit, so I'm a Questioner," or "I refuse to wash dishes, therefore I'm a Rebel," or "I love to-do lists, so I'm an Upholder." To identify our Tendency, we must consider many examples of our behavior and our *reasons* for our behaviors. For example, a Questioner and a Rebel might both reject an expectation, but the Questioner thinks, "I won't do it because it doesn't make sense," while the Rebel thinks, "I won't do it because you can't tell me what to do."

I've learned that while each of the Four Tendencies poses its difficulties, people find the Obliger and the Rebel Tendencies the most challenging—whether as a member of that Tendency themselves or dealing with that Tendency in others. (Which is why the Obliger and Rebel sections in this book are longer than the Upholder and Questioner sections.)

Many people try to map the Four Tendencies against other personality frameworks, such as the Big Five personality traits, StrengthsFinder, the Enneagram, Myers-Briggs, VIA—even onto the four houses of Hogwarts.

I'm fascinated by any scheme that helps me to understand human nature, but I think it's a mistake to try to say that "this" equals "that." Each framework captures a certain insight, and that insight would be lost if all of the systems were dumped together. No single system can capture human nature in all of its depth and variety.

Also, I think that many personality frameworks cram too many elements into their categories. By contrast, the Four Tendencies describes only one narrow aspect of a person's character—a vitally important aspect, but still just one of the multitude of qualities that form an individual. The Four Tendencies explain *why we act* and *why we don't act*.

Why It's Helpful to Identify Our Own Tendency

When I describe the Four Tendencies, I sometimes get the impression that people try to figure out the "best" Tendency and shoehorn themselves into it. But there's no best or worst Tendency. The happiest, healthiest, most productive people aren't those from a particular Tendency, but rather they're the people who have figured out how to harness the strengths of their Tendency, counteract the weaknesses, and build the lives that work for them.

With wisdom, experience, and self-knowledge from the

Four Tendencies, we can use our time more productively, make better decisions, suffer less stress, get healthier, and engage more effectively with other people.

If we don't understand our place in the Four Tendencies, however, we may fail to pinpoint the aspects of a particular situation that's causing us to succeed or fail. For instance, a literary agent told me, "I represent a journalist who did excellent work at a newspaper. No trouble with deadlines, great work ethic. But now he's on leave from the paper to write a book, and he's got writer's block."

"I bet it's not writer's block. He's probably an Obliger," I said. "He had no trouble working when he had to meet frequent deadlines. But with a distant deadline and little supervision, he can't work. He should ask his editor to check in with him every week, or join a writers' group, or you could ask him to submit pages to you every month. Just some system of external accountability."

Also, if we don't understand the Four Tendencies, we may have unrealistic assumptions of how people may change. One woman wrote, "My husband is a Rebel. I feel frustrated thinking that this is actually his character and that he'll never change. Is it possible that a Rebel is just someone who hasn't 'grown up' and realized that the world doesn't run on doing only what you 'feel like' doing at the moment? And that he will eventually change his attitude?" I didn't want to say it bluntly in my response, but gosh, no, at this point I *don't* think he'll change.

People often ask me, "Should your Tendency determine your choice of career?" Every Tendency could find a fit with just about every job, but it's interesting to think about how career and Tendency might interact. For instance, I know a professional dog trainer who is an Upholder, and he brings an Upholder spirit to it. But I can imagine how Questioners, Obligers, and Rebels could also do that work.

Even if people from each Tendency *could* pursue any career, however, that doesn't mean they *should*. The Four Tendencies can help us identify why we might enjoy certain kinds of work more—or less. One reader wrote, "Now I see why I hate my job. I am 100% Questioner, and also a tax accountant. I don't care about keeping up with the details of what's ultimately a large set of arbitrary rules that make no sense, and this has been a major hurdle in my success and happiness at work."

Knowing our own Tendency can allow us to show ourselves more compassion by realizing, "Hey, I'm this type of person, and there's nothing wrong with me. I can make the best of it." As one Upholder wrote, "My parents always told me to loosen up, my late husband always told me to loosen up, now my daughter tells me to loosen up. But now I know I'm much happier when I follow the rules that I've set for myself."

One Rebel explained:

Realizing that I'm a Rebel revealed why years of therapy failed. We'd analyzed my dearth of discipline, tried and rejected techniques that backfired (accountability? ha). It's not just that some techniques don't work for Rebels. It's that we're told (and often believe) that something is deeply wrong with us. An otherwise high-functioning, highly successful grown-up who still struggles to pay bills, complete projects, and follow through on, well, anything? Who struggles to meet everyone's expectations—even our own? That's not merely unusual; in today's world, it sounds downright pathological. But your framework assures us it's not. It's been freeing to focus on what works for me rather than what's wrong with me.

An Obliger wrote:

> As a TV writer, I've struggled miserably with my inability to stick to any kind of personal deadline, yet I've always been a dutiful employee who submits scripts on time to my boss. I've given this tendency many names: laziness, being irresponsible, being a child in grown-up clothes, and many terms that wouldn't get past your spam filter. By giving me a new name—Obliger—you've given me a way to accept myself. I can put the self-loathing aside and concentrate on devising clever ways to trick myself into doing stuff. It's already made me more productive, but more importantly, it's made me much happier.

When we recognize our Tendency, we can tweak situations to boost our chances of success. It's practically impossible to change our own nature, but it's fairly easy to change our circumstances in a way that suits our Tendency—whether by striving for more clarity, justification, accountability, or freedom. Insight about our Tendency allows us to create the situations in which we'll thrive.

Why It's Helpful to Identify Others' Tendencies

On the flip side, when we understand others' Tendencies, we're more tolerant of them. For one thing, we see that a person's behavior isn't aimed at us personally. That Questioner isn't asking questions to undermine the boss or challenge the professor's authority; the Questioner always has questions. A reader wrote, "I've lived with a Rebel for the past seven years. It's comforting to know that his way of being is as natural for *him* as being an Obliger is for *me*."

Knowing other people's Tendencies also makes it much easier to persuade them, to encourage them, and to avoid conflict. If we don't consider a person's Tendency, our words may be ineffective or even counterproductive. The fact is, if we want to communicate, we must speak the right language—not the message that would work most effectively with *us*, but the message that will persuade the *listener*. When we take into account the Four Tendencies, we can tailor our arguments to appeal to different values.

On the other hand, when we ignore the Tendencies, we lower our chances of success. The more an Upholder lectures a Rebel, the more the Rebel will want to resist. A Questioner may provide an Obliger with several sound reasons for taking an action, but those logical arguments don't matter much to an Obliger; external accountability is the key for an Obliger.

A reader sent me this hilarious list of lightbulb jokes that captures the distinctions among the Tendencies:

How do you get an Upholder to change a lightbulb?
Answer: He's already changed it.

How do you get a Questioner to change a lightbulb?
Answer: Why do we need that lightbulb anyway?

How do you get an Obliger to change a lightbulb?
Answer: Ask him to change it.

How do you get a Rebel to change a lightbulb?
Answer: Do it yourself.

A Questioner nutritionist told me, "My goal is to improve the way people eat in this country. I'm writing a book to explain how cultural and economic systems shape the way people eat." She firmly believed that if her book presented the arguments in a sufficiently logical way, people across the country would change their eating habits. Questioner!

But to communicate effectively, we must reach people through *their* Tendency, not our own. That's true for doctors, professors, coaches, bosses, spouses, parents, coworkers, teachers, neighbors, or people in any walk of life who want to persuade others to do what they want—in other words, it's true for all of us.

Even for messages meant for a wide audience, it's possible to convey information to strike a chord with every Tendency. I heard a creative example one afternoon when I spoke about the Four Tendencies at a business conference. Before introducing me, the group's head had explained, at considerable length, why it was important that participants show up on time, in the right place, for the rest of the weekend's conference activities.

After I gave my talk, I was delighted to hear him aim his reminders at each of the Four Tendencies. He said, "To you Upholders, thanks in advance for cooperating with my request for promptness. Questioners, I gave you a bunch of reasons for why you need to show up on time at all the meetings. To you Obligers, I'm watching you, and I'm counting on you to be there promptly. Rebels, save it for the bar later." *Exactly!*

Even the vocabulary we choose may resonate differently among the different Tendencies. A Rebel child might respond better if asked, "Do you feel like playing the piano now?" while an Upholder child would be happy to be reminded, "Time to practice the piano."

Just in the area of health, people's failure to listen to their doctors carries a huge cost. Poor diet, inactivity, alcohol and prescription drug abuse, and smoking are among the leading causes of illness and death in the United States—all behaviors that are within our conscious control. When we take people's Tendencies into account, we're more likely successfully to persuade them to cut back on sugar, go for a twenty-minute walk, do their rehab exercises, give up booze, or take their medications.

But it's important to remember that the Four Tendencies framework is meant to help us understand ourselves more deeply, not to limit our sense of identity or possibility. Some people say, "When you define yourself, you confine yourself." I think systems of self-definition are very helpful—because they serve as a starting point for self-knowledge. The Four Tendencies framework isn't meant to be a box that cramps our growth or a label that determines everything about us, but rather a spotlight that can illuminate hidden aspects of our nature.

When we understand ourselves and how our Tendency shapes our perspective on the world, we can adapt our circumstances to suit our own nature—and when we understand how other people's Tendencies shape *their* perspectives, we can engage with them more effectively.

With the Four Tendencies, we see how a subtle shift in vocabulary, or a quick conversation, or a minor change in procedure can be enough to change a person's entire course of action. And that matters. If this patient takes his blood-pressure medication regularly, he'll live longer. If this student completes her professor's assignments, she won't fail the course. If this husband and wife can speak to each other calmly, their marriage will last. And if I stop sending out work emails over the weekend, I won't annoy the people with whom I work.

One of the big daily challenges of life is: "How do I get people—including myself—to do what I want?" The Four Tendencies makes this task much, much easier.

2

Identify Your Tendency

Take the Four Tendencies Quiz

Of all the tasks which are set before man in life, the education and management of his character is the most important, and . . . it is necessary that he should make a calm and careful survey of his own tendencies, unblinded either by the self-deception which conceals errors and magnifies excellences, or by the indiscriminate pessimism which refuses to recognise his powers for good. He must avoid the fatalism which would persuade him that he has no power over his nature, and he must also clearly recognise that this power is not unlimited.

—William Edward Hartpole Lecky, *The Map of Life*

To identify your Tendency, take the quiz below or go to happiercast.com/quiz.

As you take the quiz, choose the answer that seems most *generally* true for you; don't search for exceptions to the rule or focus on one specific area of your life.

Getting the same number of answers for two Tendencies does *not* mean that you're a mix of those two Tendencies. Choose the one that more accurately describes you.

You're the best judge of yourself. If you believe that a different Tendency describes you better, trust yourself.

1. Have you kept a New Year's resolution where you weren't accountable to anyone—a resolution like drinking more water or keeping a journal?

a) Yes. I'm good at keeping New Year's resolutions, even the ones that no one knows about but me.

b) I'm good at keeping resolutions, but I make them whenever the time seems right. I wouldn't wait for the New Year; January 1 is an arbitrary date.

c) I've had trouble with that kind of resolution, so I'm not inclined to make one. When I'm only helping myself, I often struggle.

d) No. I hate to bind myself in any way.

2. Which statement best describes your view about your commitments to yourself?

a) I make a commitment to myself only if I'm convinced that it really makes good sense to do it.

b) If someone else is holding me accountable for my commitments, I'll meet them—but if no one knows except me, I struggle.

c) I bind myself as little as possible.

d) I take my commitments to myself as seriously as my commitments to other people.

3. At times, we feel frustrated by ourselves. Are you most likely to feel frustrated because . . .

a) My constant need for more information exhausts me.

b) As soon as I'm expected to do something, I don't want to do it.

c) I can take time for other people, but I can't take time for myself.

d) I can't take a break from my usual habits, or violate the rules, even when I want to.

4. When you've formed a healthy habit in the past, what helped you stick to it?

a) I've found it pretty easy to stick to habits, even when no one else cares.

b) I did a lot of research and customization about why and how I might keep that habit.

c) I could stick to a good habit only when I was answerable to someone else.

d) Usually I don't choose to bind myself in advance.

5. If people complain about your behavior, you'd be least surprised to hear them say . . .

a) You follow your good habits, ones that matter only to you, even when it's inconvenient for someone else.

b) You ask too many questions.

c) You're good at taking time when others ask you to do something, but you're not good at taking time for yourself.

d) You only do what you want to do, when you want to do it.

6. Which description suits you best?

a) Puts others—clients, family, neighbors, coworkers—first

b) Disciplined—sometimes, even when it doesn't make sense

c) Refuses to be bossed by others

d) Asks necessary questions

7. People get frustrated with me, because if they ask me to do something, I'm less likely to do it (even with a boss or client).
Tend to agree
Neutral
Tend to disagree

8. I do what I think makes the most sense, according to my judgment, even if that means ignoring the rules or other people's expectations.
Tend to agree
Neutral
Tend to disagree

9. Commitments to others should never be broken, but commitments to myself can be broken.
Tend to agree
Neutral
Tend to disagree

10. Sometimes I won't do something I want to do, because someone wants me to do it.
Tend to agree
Neutral
Tend to disagree

11. I've sometimes described myself as a people-pleaser.
Tend to agree
Neutral
Tend to disagree

12. I don't mind breaking rules or violating convention—I often enjoy it.

Tend to agree

Neutral

Tend to disagree

13. I question the validity of the Four Tendencies framework.

Tend to agree

Neutral

Tend to disagree

Scoring

1. a = Upholder; b = Questioner; c = Obliger; d = Rebel
2. a = Questioner; b = Obliger; c = Rebel; d = Upholder
3. a = Questioner; b = Rebel; c = Obliger; d = Upholder
4. a = Upholder; b = Questioner; c = Obliger; d = Rebel
5. a = Upholder; b = Questioner; c = Obliger; d = Rebel
6. a = Obliger; b = Upholder; c = Rebel; d = Questioner
7. "Tend to agree" indicates Rebel
8. "Tend to agree" indicates Questioner
9. "Tend to agree" indicates Obliger
10. "Tend to agree" indicates Rebel
11. "Tend to agree" indicates Obliger
12. "Tend to agree" indicates Rebel
13. "Tend to agree" indicates Questioner

UPHOLDER

"Discipline is my freedom"

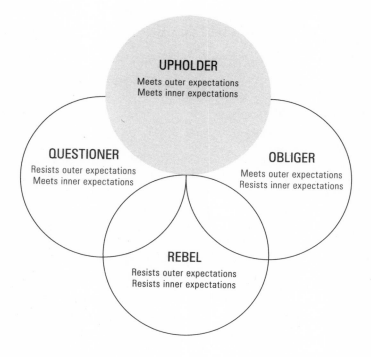

UPHOLDER
Meets outer expectations
Meets inner expectations

QUESTIONER
Resists outer expectations
Meets inner expectations

OBLIGER
Meets outer expectations
Resists inner expectations

REBEL
Resists outer expectations
Resists inner expectations

"I can do the things I want to do, and I can do the things I don't want to do."

"Why didn't you just handle it the way I told you to?"

"Your lack of planning is not my emergency."

"Do what's right even when people call you uptight."

"Just do it."

3

Understanding the Upholder

"Do what's right even when people call you uptight"

Strengths (and Weaknesses) • Weaknesses (and Strengths)
• Variations Within the Tendency • Why Upholders Have
an Instinct for Self-preservation • How Upholders Can
Manage Upholder Tightening • Why Upholders Must
Articulate Their Inner Expectations

In life, we all confront two kinds of expectations. We face the
outer expectations that others impose on us—such as submitting a report on time. We also face the *inner expectations* that
we impose on ourselves—such as going to bed every night
by 11.

In the Four Tendencies framework, Upholders are those
people who readily respond to outer and inner expectations
alike. They meet the work deadline, and they keep the New
Year's resolution, without much fuss.

For the most part, they want to do what others expect of
them—and their expectations for *themselves* are just as important.

Because of their readiness to meet outer and inner expectations, Upholders also tend to love schedules and routines—they're the people who wake up and think, "What's on my schedule and to-do list for today?" They like to know what's expected of them, and they don't like making mistakes or letting people down—including themselves.

More than the other three Tendencies, Upholders find it fairly easy to decide to act and then to follow through; they also more easily form habits.

I have a special insight into the Upholder Tendency, because this is my Tendency—which is probably why Upholder is discussed first in this framework.

In the past, I'd always assumed that most people were like me; yet at the same time I was surprised and irritated when people didn't act or think like me. So many things became clearer when I realized that a) the Four Tendencies exist, b) I'm an Upholder, and c) not many people are Upholders. It's a rare and extreme sort of personality. (By the way, no one but me was surprised to learn that I have a rare and extreme personality.)

Learning that I'm an Upholder answered a question that had long puzzled me. In my books *The Happiness Project* and *Happier at Home,* I write about the many resolutions and habits I followed to make myself happier, healthier, and more productive. After the books were published, I was struck by how many people asked me, "But how did you get yourself to *do* all those things? To write your blog posts every day, to fight right with your husband, to go to the gym?" And I'd say, "Well, I figured that these things would make me happier, so I just . . . did them." "But *how?*" they'd repeat. I couldn't understand why people seemed so hung up on this question.

Now I understand. For an Upholder like me, it's not hard to decide to act and then to follow through. For many people, it's not as simple.

Strengths (and Weaknesses)

I can say from personal experience—and of course I'm biased—that there are many terrific aspects of Upholderness. Other people can rely on Upholders, and Upholders can rely on themselves.

Upholders readily meet outer expectations. They're self-directed and have little trouble hitting deadlines, keeping appointments, meeting commitments, or managing tasks—and they don't depend on supervision, oversight, reminders, or penalties to stay on track.

Upholders are often very intrigued by rules. For example, even if I'm just passing through, if I see a list of regulations—posted by a swimming pool or in an office kitchen—I can't resist reading and following them. We Upholders usually don't mind wearing a uniform, following a precise recipe, or obeying instructions.

Just as Upholders readily meet outer expectations, they meet inner expectations. If Upholders decide to do something, they do it—even when other people don't care, and sometimes, even when other people are inconvenienced.

As a result, as an Upholder, I know that I can count on myself. I can count on myself more than I can count on any other person in my life.

Almost always, if I make a commitment, I can stick to it, even without outside help. Back when I was on a legal career track, I had to take the bar exam. To prepare, I ordered a collection of BARBRI review cassette tapes and spent hours listening, taking notes, and studying—in my own kitchen. My friends opted to attend BARBRI classes to help them stick to the study schedule, but I could do it on my own.

Because of their desire to meet outer and inner expectations, Upholders are independent and reliable, and they have a high degree of self-mastery. If they tell you that they're going to do something, they do it.

In fact, because Upholders readily meet expectations, non-Upholders sometimes try to piggyback on Upholders' self-accountability. One Upholder wrote:

> I wondered why, whenever I started a diet, exercise regimen, or hobby, I'd attract people who wanted to join me. I realized they wanted me to provide them with support: "Call me when you're going for a bike ride, and I'll meet you at the park." Now I understand that they were trying to coast on my willpower because they needed the commitment with me to get themselves going.

In my own experience, while it's sometimes satisfying to help other people meet their expectations, more often I wish they wouldn't rely on me to keep pushing things forward.

For Upholders, meeting outer and inner expectations doesn't make them feel trapped; it makes them feel creative and free, because they can execute any plan they want. If I decide—as I did—that I wanted to write a short book over the summer or that I wanted to quit sugar, I know I'll follow through, even if no one else cares. That certainty about myself gives me a deep sense of freedom, control, and possibility.

However, I don't want to give the impression that Upholders never struggle to meet expectations. We do. I have to fight to maintain some of my good habits like going to the gym, making phone calls, or running errands. I procrastinate, I slip up. But for the most part, it's easier for Upholders to meet expectations than it is for the other Tendencies.

Upholders readily meet outer and inner rules, and they also often search for the rules beyond the rules—as in ethics or morals. For instance, one of the most famous Upholders is certainly Hermione Granger from J. K. Rowling's Harry Potter series. Hermione never falls behind on her homework, constantly reminds Harry and Ron about the regulations of the magical world, and becomes anxious when anyone steps out of line. Nevertheless, when she believes that conventional expectations are unjust, she crusades against them—she sees the rules beyond the rules—even in the face of others' indifference or outright disapproval. She campaigns to improve the poor treatment of house-elves, and she quits school and opposes the Ministry of Magic to fight the evil Voldemort. She eagerly meets society's rules and laws until they conflict with her own inner sense of justice—at which point she rejects them.

(I love the Harry Potter books, in part because I love seeing an Upholder uphold in such an admirable way. I wonder if that's true for everyone—are we all particularly drawn to depictions of our own Tendency?)

Because Upholders easily meet both outer and inner expectations, they rarely suffer from resentment or burnout, and they don't depend on others to motivate or supervise them. While their discipline may make them appear rigid to others, Upholders themselves feel free, effective, and independent.

Weaknesses (and Strengths)

As with all the Tendencies, the Upholders' strengths can become weaknesses.

The Upholder can become the fearless campaigner for justice, or the hanging judge who blindly enforces the law, or the tattletale schoolchild who reports every minor infraction by the other kids, or the boss who rejects the report because it's submitted an hour late.

Because of their affinity for meeting expectations, Upholders may feel compelled to observe rules even when it's more sensible to ignore them. Although I have no problem using a unisex bathroom, I can't make myself use a restroom marked MEN, even if it's a single-occupant room. An Upholder friend told me, "On my way to the hospital to give birth, I told my husband not to speed, and I insisted that he park in the correct lot, even though I wound up giving birth less than twenty minutes after we pulled in."

Upholders sometimes become impatient—or even disdainful—when people reject expectations, can't impose expectations on themselves, or question expectations. An Obliger reader wrote, "I told a coworker that I can't take vitamins because it's hard to stick to it without external accountability. She said 'Grow up.'" Yep, sounds like an Upholder. Not a very *nice* Upholder, but an Upholder.

As an Upholder, I want others not merely to meet expectations but to *want* to meet them. I like to cross items off a to-do list, meet self-imposed deadlines, and follow instructions, and for a long time it perplexed me when others didn't feel the same way. Now I realize that I'm being even more demanding because of my desire not to be demanding.

Upholders can become disapproving and uneasy when others misbehave, even in minor ways. I get tense if someone starts whispering to me during a meeting. At the same time, my Upholderness can bring out my rude side. I don't mean to be brusque or pushy, but I'm so worried about being late, or not following instructions correctly, that I may lose my courtesy.

Upholders may find it difficult to delegate because they doubt others' ability to follow through. "I'm married to an Upholder," one reader wrote. "On Sundays, she writes out index cards for each day of the week and does an amazing job of checking off her lists. She takes care of our kids, grandkids, parents, her sister, etc. One of her common refrains is: 'Why can't anybody in this family get their own sh$% done?'"

Nevertheless—perhaps surprisingly—Upholders often resist holding others accountable, even when people *ask* for accountability. Because Upholders don't need much outer accountability themselves, they're not sympathetic when others do. Also, because Upholders feel the pressure of outer accountability themselves, they don't like to place that burden on others. I know that I'm reluctant—sometimes to a fault—to prod people, including my own children, to act. I should remind my daughters to make their beds, to use better table manners, to read more—but I can't face the prospect of reminding them, checking on them, and then reminding them again.

Upholders may feel uneasy about changes to routines, habits, or schedules. Recently, my husband, Jamie, and I were in Boston for a wedding, and the invitation instructed: "The bus will leave the hotel for the church at 6:00 p.m." At breakfast, the bride's mother told us, "Actually, the bus will leave at 5:45."

"But the card said 6:00," I said.

"Yes, but now it's leaving at 5:45. Traffic."

As Jamie and I walked away, I said to him, "How can they change it? The card says 6:00!" (As a Questioner, Jamie wasn't as disturbed by this change as I was.)

To others, the ways of the Upholder can seem extreme. I know an Upholder who carries index cards in a special wallet: green for today's to-do list; pink for this week's to-do list; yellow for work-related items not captured on the green and pink cards; and white for personal items. "When people see this system, they think I'm a bit psycho," he admitted. (Maybe an inclination to use index cards is a clue that someone's an Upholder.)

To others, the Upholder commitment to inner and outer expectations can sometimes seem cold and inflexible. One reader wrote:

> I've found many Upholders to be rigid in following their own expectations, even when it would make sense to accommodate others, if they don't have time to adjust to new circumstances. For example, an Upholder says, "We've planned to drive our own car and leave at X time, and no, we can't adapt that plan to pick up another person." I have many friends who are working moms, and the Obligers are always the ones who are flexible and creative in helping each other juggle schedules and kids, while the Upholders often give off the vibe of "We've planned everything in advance and can't modify to help anyone else at this point." They're reliable and predictable, but in many situations, it's a plus to be more adaptable.

Very true. We Upholders find it tough to change plans at the last minute—especially when we're thinking, "Why didn't you figure out this car-pooling problem yesterday?"

I love being an Upholder, but I see its dark side, too. I'm very good at getting myself to do things that I don't want to do—sometimes, too good. I can spend time and energy on something just because I think I "should," without questioning enough.

But I still do love being an Upholder.

Variations Within the Tendency

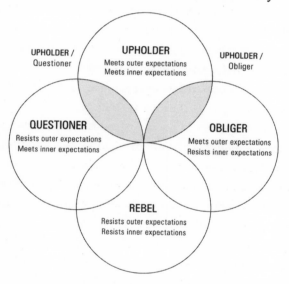

As with all the Tendencies, Upholders come in a wide variety. People's personalities differ in many ways—an Upholder might be very ambitious, intelligent, anxious, sociable, volatile, loving, or creative, mixed in with his or her Upholder qualities.

Moreover, each Tendency interlocks with two other Tendencies, and a person of a particular Tendency often "tips" in the direction of one of the overlapping Tendencies. In the case of Upholders, the Upholder overlaps with the Questioner (both meet inner expectations) and the Obliger (both meet outer expectations).

UPHOLDER/Questioners find it easier to question external expectations and are therefore better able to consider rejecting them: "My boss says I have to go on that trip, but is it really necessary?" They also more easily question the value of an inner expectation. I remember a conversation I had with myself about an inner expectation: "I've been meditating every morning for months, and it doesn't seem to be doing any good. Should I quit the habit?" I was able to say, "Yes, it's time to quit." (Note, however, that as an Upholder, I had already stuck with it for several months.)

Upholders-tipped-to-Questioners are more willing to reject the prevailing expectations of society. And if a conflict arises between outer and inner expectations, UPHOLDER/Questioners give greater weight to inner expectations—as Questioners do. "Tomorrow, we're all giving our presentations, and my coworker wants me to give him a critique, but I need time to work on my own presentation, so I'll tell him I can't do it."

On the other side, UPHOLDER/Obligers tip toward responding to outer expectations. For UPHOLDER/Obligers, the burden of outer expectations feels heavier, and if there's a conflict, outer expectations may more easily trump inner expectations. Such UPHOLDER/Obligers may struggle to set limits, and at the extreme end, they may even show UPHOLDER/Obliger-rebellion. For the most part, they easily meet inner and outer goals, but every once in a while they "snap"—failing to give themselves a needed break, which most Upholders can do, and then explosively refusing to meet an expectation.

At a party, I had a long discussion with a novelist friend about whether she was an Upholder or an Obliger. We couldn't figure out the answer that night, so she emailed me the next morning:

> I'll eat things I don't want to eat, and suffer through events that are torture for me, and not contradict people who are borderline offensive. But I'm also very disciplined about my writing and my exercise and my reading, and get a lot accomplished *as long as* my pursuits don't get in anyone's way. I manage this by carving out large chunks of solitary time where I'm off the grid and unaccountable. I know myself and have built myself a strong protective mechanism: a lot of childcare and an office space away from home.

From this description, I pegged her as a highly considerate UPHOLDER/Obliger. She's able to meet inner expectations without outer accountability, but only when outer expectations don't interfere. Though Upholders-tipped-to-Obligers have a commitment to both inner and outer expectations, for them, the pull of outer expectations is very hard to ignore; UPHOLDER/Obligers must be sure to articulate inner expectations and to create boundaries to protect inner expectations from outer interference.

Some Upholders explain their determination to meet their inner expectations by saying it's necessary to strengthen themselves to meet others' expectations. When asked for a Tendency motto, one Upholder suggested, "If I want to support others, I must first support myself." That's the view of an UPHOLDER/Obliger. As an UPHOLDER/Questioner, I don't feel the need to justify myself. I meet my inner expectations because they're important to me.

Why Upholders Have an Instinct
for Self-preservation

Because they meet both outer and inner expectations, it might seem likely that of the Four Tendencies, Upholders would feel most burdened by the weight of expectations. Not so. *Obligers* feel most burdened. While Upholders and Obligers both meet external expectations, Upholders also meet their expectations for themselves, and this protects them from the resentment and burnout that often trouble Obligers.

Although it might seem counterintuitive, most Upholders are good at taking care of themselves and enjoying themselves. For instance, one study of Facebook status updates showed that people who scored high on "conscientiousness" (good at planning and getting things done) also wrote a lot about getting rest and enjoying leisure—they frequently used words like "weekend" and "relaxing."

That's because Upholders use their Upholderness to schedule time for leisure; "goof off" becomes an item on the to-do list. One listener remarked, "During the year my wife gave herself to write her dissertation, she woke up every morning at 5:00 a.m. and went to work. By 4 p.m. she was ready to go to the gym and quit for the day. There was an amazing lack of drama. She's also very interested in having fun, so her Upholder Tendency seems mostly like overly aggressive cruise-directing."

Upholders are also good at ignoring others' expectations in order to meet their own inner expectations and to be self-protective. I was invited to dinner at an Upholder friend's house, and at a certain time, he stood up and said, "Okay, everybody out. I need to get to sleep." In the elevator, another friend said, "Wow, it was kind of amazing that he just kicked us all out. Don't you think that was rude?" Maybe it was—but to me, as a fellow Upholder, it seemed perfectly reasonable.

Upholders seek to maintain a high level of self-mastery and performance—which is one reason they take such satisfaction in sticking to their good habits. Upholders value self-command, so they tend to pay a lot of attention to getting enough sleep, exercising, having fun, keeping gas in the car, and so on. In fact, in the representative sample I studied, Upholders were far more likely to say, "I'm good at sticking to habits, even when no one else cares."

People often give the advice "Don't be so hard on yourself," or "It's not healthy to be so inflexible," or "No one else is paying any attention to that rule," but for Upholders, meeting outer and inner expectations is very gratifying. This feeling is sometimes very hard for others—especially Rebels—to grasp. I remember talking to a Rebel friend about it.

"For me," I explained, "discipline brings freedom."

"But discipline means limits," she said. "Who wants to follow the rules?"

"I give myself limits to give myself freedom."

She shook her head. "That doesn't make sense. Freedom means no limits. I want to do what I want to do."

We looked at each other and started laughing. Neither of us was going to convert the other, that was clear.

Along the same lines, I've noticed that when people in the other Tendencies want to comfort or treat themselves, they often excuse themselves from an expectation. They might think, "After the tough day I've had, I'm going to skip my CrossFit class." But as an Upholder, I find that letting myself off the hook usually makes me feel *worse*.

Perhaps the Upholder emphasis on self-command accounts

for an interesting result in the representative sample. Of the Four Tendencies, at 24%, Upholders were the least likely to agree with the statement "I have struggled with addiction." The other three Tendencies scored about the same (34%, 32%, 32%), so it seems likely that there's something specific to Upholders' nature that protects them.

In fact, the Upholder commitment to meeting expectations can sometimes make Upholders seem . . . *cold.* There's a relentless quality to Upholders. They're going to do what must be done even, sometimes, if that means inconveniencing other people or being out of step.

My Obliger sister, Elizabeth, and I have a weekly podcast, *Happier with Gretchen Rubin,* and we devoted episodes 35, 36, 37, and 38 to the Four Tendencies. When we were talking about Upholders, Elizabeth noted, "Well, Gretch, being your sister, I've had a lifetime of seeing both the strengths and the weaknesses of you being an Upholder." She told a story from a few years ago when our two families took a trip together. At the last minute, Jamie and my older daughter Eliza couldn't go, so my younger daughter, Eleanor, and I met Elizabeth, her husband, Adam, and her son, Jack, at a resort not far from their house in Los Angeles.

"We were in L.A., on West Coast time," Elizabeth recalled, "and you decided that you and Eleanor should stay on East Coast time. Every night, you two ate dinner at about 4:30 p.m., and then went to bed at 7:30—and meanwhile, Adam, Jack, and I had a whole separate vacation, from 7 p.m. to midnight."

"That's right!" I said.

"See, to me, it seems like you miss out on fun and relaxation that way."

I could see her point, but when I thought about the agony

of trying to stay awake during dinner and then having to readjust when we returned home—well, it just didn't seem worth it.

After the episode aired, I was fascinated by the response from a listener who took a dim view of my approach—and who, I strongly suspect, is an Obliger. She argued not that my approach would diminish *my* enjoyment of the vacation—which was Elizabeth's point to me—but that my approach would take away from *other people's* enjoyment. She wrote:

> It seemed like you thought it was perfectly okay to stay on East Coast time. By sticking to your schedule and staying rigid because you're an Upholder, you may actually be spoiling other people's vacations. I felt that there was a lack of awareness on your part. Rather than really be in the moment with Elizabeth and her family, who had set aside the time to be with you and your daughter, you put your own schedule first.

I wrote back:

> You point out that Elizabeth and her family had set aside time to be with us. Absolutely true! Likewise, we put aside our time to be with them.
>
> In fact, we flew to L.A. from N.Y.C., no small undertaking, so that they could stay within an easy, close drive of their house. So would it have been equally reasonable to expect them to stick to our time zone for two days? To eat breakfast and dinner on our schedule?
>
> In my view, it's not that one person is "right" but just that people are coming from different perspectives.

In fact, though it sounds a bit callous to admit it, as an Upholder I often wish that the people around me would take care of themselves the way that I take care of myself, so that I wouldn't have to worry about their comfort or convenience. I absolutely understood the boyfriend's perspective when an Obliger wrote, "My Upholder boyfriend sometimes feels that I'm too needy—rather than doing what would make me happy, I often wait to hear what would make *him* happy and then decide to do that. As much as you'd think someone would appreciate having their happiness put first, he actually prefers that I do what I want for myself, first and foremost."

Although Upholders take great satisfaction in their routines and their good habits, to someone on the outside, their disciplined approach can make them look like a killjoy. I suspect that Upholders in the entertainment business, and in the arts, sometimes go out of their way to hide their Tendency—to present themselves as more wild and hedonistic than they actually are. Upholderness isn't a very glamorous, edgy, or endearing quality. It doesn't contribute to a fascinating biography or make good publicity copy. In her megahit song "Shake It Off," Taylor Swift sings about how she stays up too late and dates too many guys—but *does* she stay up too late? Hmmm. I wonder. Taylor Swift sure looks like an Upholder to me.

How Upholders Can Manage Upholder Tightening

Although Upholders generally show a strong instinct for self-preservation, their Upholder nature does sometimes lead to the pattern of "tightening."

When people in the other three Tendencies try to meet expectations, they tend to start off strong and then slacken over time. They look for loopholes, they find exceptions, they become less conscientious. This happens to me, too, with some habits. But sometimes, Upholders can have the reverse experience—a kind of *tightening*. It becomes harder for them to make an exception, to take a break, to lighten up. That can be good—but it can also be bad.

An Upholder friend had a lot of muscle pain, and I convinced her to try my strength-training gym. She already exercised regularly, but I thought this particular regimen might help her. So she went, and she cured her pain, and then she wanted to stop going, because the gym was located in a very inconvenient place for her, and she got regular exercise elsewhere. But although she said she wanted to stop, she couldn't seem to. Her Upholder nature had locked in and wouldn't release. Another Upholder told me in mock despair: "I kept increasing my daily Fitbit steps goal until I was literally jogging beside the bed before I would get in, just to reach the target." That's tightening.

Tightening can happen in any context. One Upholder experienced work tightening. "During a particularly busy time at work, I started going into the office at 7:00 a.m. (we officially start at 9:00). It's settled down now, yet I still go in at that time. Mostly I enjoy it, but I'd also love the flexibility to be able to feel okay about going in later if, for instance, I wanted to have breakfast with my husband."

So how can Upholders combat troublesome tightening? By staying alert for the tightening pattern, and when it strikes, considering carefully whether that expectation deserves to be met. Upholders can remind themselves that at a certain point, following tighter and tighter expectations undermines performance and self-mastery. And as always, Upholders must make sure to articulate their inner expectations.

One of my favorite writers, the eighteenth-century essayist and lexicographer Samuel Johnson, observed, "All severity that does not tend to increase good, or prevent evil, is idle." An important reminder for Upholders.

Why Upholders Must Articulate Their Inner Expectations

Although Upholders can indeed reject outer expectations in order to meet inner expectations, they don't always have a clear sense of what they expect from themselves. *For an inner expectation to be met, it must be clearly articulated.* Therefore, Upholders must take care to define for themselves what they want and what they value—that clarity is essential.

I know this very well from my own experience. After college, I wasn't sure what career to follow. I figured law school would be a great education, it would prepare me for many different careers, and I could always change my mind about my career choice later. Right? So I went to law school.

Law school is very attractive to Upholders: it's very clear how to apply and how to succeed once you're there, and the very point of law school is to understand and follow the rules. I met those outer expectations, and I did very well. In law school, I became the editor in chief of Yale's law review, I won a writing prize, and I got a clerkship with Justice Sandra Day O'Connor.

During my clerkship, however, I realized for the first time that I really wanted to be a writer.

Once that inner expectation kicked in, I had no trouble

abandoning my legal career and starting over from scratch—without any deadlines or accountability. "But how did you do it?" people often ask. "How did you have the discipline to write a proposal, work on a book, and get an agent, all on your own?" For me, once I'd clearly heard the voice of my own inner expectation, doing the work wasn't hard. *But it took me a long time to hear that voice.*

SUMMARY: UPHOLDER

LIKELY STRENGTHS:

Self-starter

Self-motivated

Conscientious

Reliable

Thorough

Sticks to a schedule

Eager to understand and meet expectations

POSSIBLE WEAKNESSES:

Defensive

Rigid

Often struggles when plans or schedules change

Can seem humorless and uptight

Uneasy when rules are ambiguous or undefined

Impatient when others need reminders,
deadlines, supervision, or discussion

Demanding

May become anxious about obeying
rules that don't even exist

4

Dealing with an Upholder

"Just do it"

Work • Spouse • Child • Health Client • Choosing a Career

Dealing with an Upholder at Work

Upholders can make great colleagues; they're self-starters, they're very interested in performance, they don't need supervision, and they're good at recognizing their limits.

Also, for others, it's energizing to work with people who execute everything they've promised; other people know that if an Upholder says he'll do it, it gets done. A boss can say to an Upholder, "When you have a chance, can you look into this issue and tell me what you find?" and make no further mention of the assignment, then six weeks later get a full report from the Upholder.

They can make great bosses because they're clear about setting expectations and are highly disciplined themselves. An Upholder boss would be clear about what's expected from a particular position, fair about enforcing rules and schedules, and far-sighted in following a long process toward a conclusion; an Upholder boss wouldn't suddenly change goals, methods, or deadlines.

Upholders do well as entrepreneurs or freelancers, or with any kind of side hustle, because they're self-motivated. They can identify what needs to be done and then follow through, even when they don't have a client, customer, or boss to hold them accountable. In analyzing the results of my nationally representative survey, I was interested to see that as a person's income rises, he or she is more likely to be an Upholder (and less likely to be a Rebel).

However, Upholders sometimes get impatient when others struggle to meet expectations. An Upholder boss may resist answering Questioners' questions, saying, "We got a memo about the new deadline from Corporate, and I'm sure they have a good reason for changing it; let's stop arguing about it and get to work." An Upholder boss may resist building in the systems of accountability needed by Obligers—such as setting deadlines or enforcing vacation days—because he or she doesn't understand why it's necessary. Working with Rebel employees will very likely be a real challenge (for both sides).

Upholders get frustrated by others' failure to meet expectations. One Upholder explained:

> I'm an Upholder doctor in a busy subspecialty medical practice, and my partners are Questioners and Rebels. They tend to set rules for our practice that may be unrealistic, and as an Upholder, I feel greatly stressed when these rules get bent or broken. Often, I'm the only one following these rules, or even worse, I'm put in the uncomfortable position of policing my senior partners when they fail to meet the expectations that they claim to endorse for all of us. I'm going to

advocate that instead of making rules, we use our best judgment on a case-by-case basis.

Upholders sometimes have trouble delegating, because they assume that others will drop the ball or won't do a good job.

At times, Upholders can become locked in to routines and schedules, and they may find it hard to disregard rules, even senseless rules, and may not recognize when it's time to make changes. Upholders may find it hard to drop a pointless expectation or take a break. They also may have trouble accommodating change on short notice, so those around them should strive to give them plenty of advance warning about any change or new assignment.

For people managing Upholders, it's helpful to remember that because they hate to fail to meet an expectation, they may find it hard to set priorities—all expectations seem equally important. To counter this, a boss or colleague should make priorities clear: "Usually I want that report every Friday, but when the annual report is due, it's okay to put off the weekly report while we finish the annual report. The annual report is more important."

Because of the Upholder desire to meet both inner and outer expectations, Upholders may be reluctant to pitch in to help others if it means setting aside their own obligations.

Upholders get very upset when they do make mistakes or break commitments—sometimes, too upset. An Upholder friend is an editor at a major newspaper. "I really, really hate it when there's a mistake in a story that I worked on," she told me. "Other people seem to take it in stride, but I feel terrible." A comment such as "It's no big deal" or "No one even noticed" is less helpful to such a person than "You tried your hardest, and that's the best anyone can do." Because they hate to screw up, Upholders can be very defensive or hostile when told they've made a mistake.

Because Upholders want to meet expectations, they may refuse to tackle a new opportunity if they're afraid they won't be able to fulfill it. Of course, sometimes this is helpful, because it means Upholders are good at drawing boundaries, but sometimes it's not helpful, when they don't challenge themselves, for fear that they won't be able to "do it right."

Dealing with an Upholder Spouse

Upholders—like people in all the Four Tendencies—can't turn their personalities on and off. In many ways, it's great to be married to an Upholder, but on the other hand, an Upholder is likely to want to work during a vacation or to practice the violin even when guests are visiting for the weekend.

When we understand a person's Tendency, we're able to understand his or her perspective. An Upholder friend told me how the Tendencies helped her avoid a fight with her husband.

"We were taking the train to visit my parents. Our son had turned twelve years old the day before, so instead of being 75 cents, his ticket cost $8.50. But I thought, 'If we don't pay full fare, it will ruin my weekend.'"

"Right," I said, nodding.

"But my husband is a Questioner. He thought I was being too extreme. He said, 'It's arbitrary, he's just one day older, so it's fair to buy the cheaper ticket.'"

"Which makes sense from his point of view," I acknowledged. "And a Rebel might think, 'Hah! Metro-North can't make me pay.'"

Understanding fosters tolerance.

Upholders tend to dislike changing plans or being spontaneous. In my own marriage, Jamie refuses to answer my questions, which I think is partly due to his Questioner nature and partly due to his desire to avoid creating a specific expectation in me, his Upholder wife. If he tells me that we should leave for the party at 7:00 p.m. but then decides that we should leave at 7:15, I may resist that change. If he doesn't tell me until I absolutely need to know, he spares himself that possible conflict.

Upholders may feel pressure to meet an expectation, even if it doesn't make sense in a particular circumstance—which can annoy their partners. To argue most effectively, a spouse does well to acknowledge Upholder values. A spouse might say, "I see that the sign says 'Authorized Personnel Only,' but I think we qualify as 'authorized personnel' here," or "The form says that it's due by June 1, but this company wants our money, and the actual date is September, so I think it's fine if we send in the form on June 15."

The spouse of an Upholder should guard against suggesting a possible expectation because the Upholder may embrace it—even when it's not a good idea. A spouse's mere passing thought—"You should run to be the head of the neighborhood association," "You'd make a great chair for the church committee," or "You should reorganize your employees into a more effective structure"—might lock in tight around the Upholder.

The spouse of an Upholder can help by providing reminders of inner expectations, such as "You don't have to do that," "Is this important to you?" or "You did your best, you made a mistake, it happens."

Upholders can become impatient when their spouses don't readily meet expectations. Questioners married to

Upholders may need to remind them that as Questioners, they need reasons; Obligers, that they need accountability; Rebels, that they need choice and freedom.

Dealing with an Upholder Child

In most ways, the parents of Upholder children have an easy time. Upholder children want to understand and meet expectations, and they're self-motivated. Parents don't have to be involved in many homework battles or remind a child to feed a fish. An Upholder child will practice the piano without many reminders, plan ahead to pack the right soccer equipment, and keep track of the school schedule.

Parents enjoy this aspect of Upholderness, but they may get frustrated when a child can't turn off the Upholder Tendency. From time to time, they want the child to loosen up or let go of expectations. Not likely. The Upholder child may go nuts if he can't do the thirty minutes of reading that he's supposed to do before bed or if she arrives five minutes late for school.

As with all the Tendencies, arguments work better when they address that Tendency's values. A parent might explain, "Your teacher expects you to read for thirty minutes every night, but because we went to visit Grandma, it will be bedtime by the time we get home. A good night's sleep will make you alert for school tomorrow, and that's more important than reading tonight." Or: "The teacher understands that sometimes children can't complete an assignment, for reasons that aren't their fault, and that's okay." Those arguments will work better than arguments such as "You deserve it," "The teacher won't know that you skipped one day," "The teacher isn't the boss of you," or "Reading for thirty minutes is just an arbitrary goal," which are far less persuasive to an Upholder.

Upholder children may also find it hard to change schedules suddenly, to leave a task unfinished if it's time to move on, or to handle situations where expectations aren't clear.

While most parents would find it fairly easy to have an Upholder child, the parent-child relationship between an Upholder and a Rebel is often difficult to manage, on both sides.

Like spouses of Upholders, parents of Upholder children should guard against accidentally introducing an expectation or suggesting unnecessary rules. It's easy for an Upholder to lock on to an expectation and spend tremendous energy and time living up to it, even if it's not something that he or she wants to do—or even a good idea. A casual comment like "You should enter the spelling bee" might set off an enormous and unintended chain reaction.

The adults around an Upholder child should help that child to articulate his or her own inner expectations so that inner as well as outer expectations can be achieved.

Dealing with an Upholder Patient or Health Client

For doctors and other health-care providers, Upholders make easy patients. They take doctors' orders seriously, they take their pills as directed, they're rigorous about doing physical therapy.

So in the representative sample I studied, I wasn't surprised to see that of all the four Tendencies, Upholders—at 70%—were the most likely to disagree with the statement

"My doctor has told me why it's important that I make a certain change in my life, but I haven't done it."

In fact, Upholders may have the opposite problem—they may too readily follow a doctor's instructions and fail to ask enough questions. When I was twenty years old, an orthodontist casually told me, "Your jaw needs to be broken and reset. You have no pain or symptoms now, but mark my words, by thirty you'll be experiencing chronic jaw pain." I managed to question this advice, but it took every ounce of my strength. (I still haven't had any jaw problems, by the way.)

Health-care professionals should remember that Upholders tend to meet expectations faithfully, and may even experience tightening, so it's not helpful to exaggerate standards in order to get adherence. At the same time, Upholders' instinct for self-preservation helps them speak up when expectations become too burdensome. When I switched to a new trainer at my high-intensity weight-training gym, I had no trouble telling him, "You're making the weights too heavy. I want them very heavy, but this is just too intense for me."

Choosing a Career as an Upholder

Thinking about Tendency and career isn't a simple matter of "Upholders should work as bank regulators or traffic cops, because they'd enforce rules all day." Just about every job could be done by a different Tendency, in that Tendency's own way, but it's true that certain circumstances tend to favor—or not—different Tendencies.

Upholders do well in roles that require people to be self-starters, such as starting a business, solo consulting, or freelancing, because once they decide to meet an aim, they can work toward it without supervision or accountability. Upholders have a deep capacity to make themselves do things they don't feel like doing, which is invaluable for people who work for themselves and lack coworkers to help with the details or drudge work.

Upholders tend to thrive in situations where the rules are clear, because they take great satisfaction in fulfilling expectations. They might struggle in an environment where it's important to be able to change course abruptly or adapt quickly to changing schedules or expectations. One Upholder explained, "I'm an Upholder, which makes me great at finding out the rules and making sure that people stick to them. But flexibility is really valued in my workplace, which I'm not so good at."

And they might be uneasy in an area where expectations aren't clear, where rules are ambiguous—or where they're expected to stretch the rules. The boss wants a general counsel who will interpret tax laws aggressively and creatively? Don't hire an Upholder.

I've noticed that Upholders are sometimes drawn to occupations where they help people with performance—I know an Upholder who's a high-level coach, for instance, and several Upholders (like me) who write books about people improving performance, self-management, or habits.

However, because Upholders easily meet outer and inner expectations, they're often perplexed when other people just can't "do it already," and they may not have helpful advice. One Upholder wrote, "I'm a personal trainer. Good: I definitely model the workout/nutrition lifestyle that I hope my clients will adopt, and I'm always on time. Not-so-good: I sometimes get frustrated when clients aren't as dedicated as I would want them to be."

At a dinner, I was seated next to the CEO of a major bio-pharmaceutical company, and as often happens, I couldn't resist describing the Four Tendencies. He grasped them immediately.

"I'm an Upholder," he told me, "and I bet that most of my fellow CEOs are Upholders, too."

"Why?" I asked.

"Because to be the CEO of a public company, you have to be comfortable with following the rules and meeting enormous expectations from others. And you also have to feel self-directed, you have to be able to steer your own course and tell people no."

An Upholder friend, an investment banker, joined in the conversation. "I think that's right. Like an Obliger makes a great number two—"

"My number two is an Obliger, and he's outstanding," the first man interjected.

"—but a good CEO has to be able to say, 'I care what other people think, but in the end, I know what I want to do.' And it takes tremendous discipline to have that kind of role—the kind that's possible only when inner and outer expectations coincide, so that there's no resentment, no inner conflict."

"I don't know that I agree," I said, shaking my head. "I think all four Tendencies can be terrific leaders, in their own ways."

"Questioners and Rebels would make great founders and innovators," the CEO acknowledged. "But I think they'd struggle to build a mature company. Take a Rebel. As a public CEO, there's too much scrutiny, right down to how you dress, how you talk to the Board."

At first, I was convinced—but then I thought, "Well,

three Upholders deciding that only Upholders could be good public CEOs?" I wondered if three Questioners or three Obligers would conclude the same thing about their own Tendency. Rebels—well, I think it's likely that even a Rebel would acknowledge that it's a rare Rebel who would make a successful CEO for a public company.

SUMMARY: DEALING WITH
AN UPHOLDER

They readily meet external and internal expectations

They're self-directed, so they can meet deadlines, work on projects, and take the initiative without much supervision

They enjoy routine and may have trouble adjusting to a break in routine or sudden scheduling changes

They hate to make mistakes, and because of that . . .

They may become very angry or defensive at the suggestion that they've dropped the ball or made a mistake

They put a high value on follow-through

They may need to be reminded that, unlike them, others aren't necessarily comforted or energized by getting things done

They may have trouble delegating responsibilities, because they suspect that others aren't dependable

QUESTIONER

"I'll comply—if you convince me why"

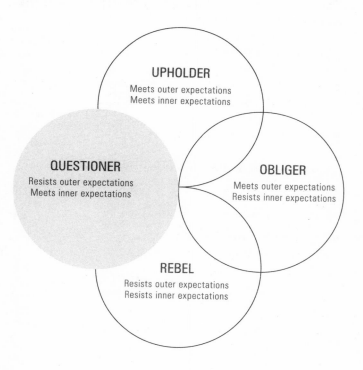

UPHOLDER
Meets outer expectations
Meets inner expectations

QUESTIONER
Resists outer expectations
Meets inner expectations

OBLIGER
Meets outer expectations
Resists inner expectations

REBEL
Resists outer expectations
Resists inner expectations

"I'll comply—if you convince me why."

"PROVE IT."

"'Because i said so'? I don't think so!"

"Don't lose sight of why."

"Blind obedience is
servitude. Or is it?"

"Wait, what?"

"Justification leads to motivation."

*"Seek and seek and seek and seek—
and maybe ye shall find."*

"Optimizing life—even
when we don't want to."

"But why?"

"IT'S MY WAY OR THE WRONG WAY."

"Why do we need a motto?"

5

Understanding the Questioner

"But why?"

Strengths (and Weaknesses) • Weaknesses (and Strengths)
• Variations Within the Tendency • Why Questioners
Dislike Being Questioned • How Questioners Can Master
Analysis-Paralysis • How Questioners Can Meet Unjustified
Expectations by Finding Their Own Justifications

At work, at home, and in life, we all confront both *outer* and *inner* expectations. While Upholders readily meet both outer and inner expectations, Questioners meet only inner expectations—and that includes outer expectations that they've turned into inner expectations.

In accepting those inner expectations, Questioners show a deep commitment to information, logic, and efficiency. They want to gather their own facts, decide for themselves, and act with good reason; they object to anything they consider arbitrary, ill-reasoned, ill-informed, or ineffective. Many, many people are Questioners; only the Obliger Tendency has more members.

For Questioners, how do outer expectations become

inner expectations? Questioners meet an expectation only if they endorse it as efficient and reasonable. For instance, a Questioner thinks, "My father keeps reminding me to get my oil checked, but I don't think that's necessary now—so I'll ignore him," or "The sign above the office kitchen sink says that we're supposed to do our own dishes, but washing mugs isn't a productive use of my time; it's more efficient to let the night staff wash up. So I'll leave my mug here in the sink."

On the other hand, a Questioner readily meets an outer expectation that's well justified because it then becomes an inner expectation. A Questioner thinks, "My teacher explained that I'll finish my math homework more quickly once I've memorized the multiplication tables, so I want to get that done," or "My wife has wanted me to clean out the guest room for months, but we never use the guest room, so I refused to do it. Now that we have guests coming in a few weeks, I'll do it."

Because of their focus on justification, Questioners wake up each day and think, "What needs to get done today and why?" They decide for themselves whether or not a course of action is a good idea. If the boss tells a Questioner to finish the report by this Friday, the Questioner might decide, "No one is going to read the report until next Wednesday, and it's more efficient for me to write it at the beginning of the week, so I'll finish it by Wednesday." No surprise, in the representative sample, Questioner was the Tendency most likely to agree with the statement "I do what I think makes the most sense, according to my judgment, even if that means ignoring the rules or other people's expectations."

Once Questioners accept the reasons for an expectation, they're self-directed and don't need much supervision. So for a boss trying to persuade a Questioner to use a new billing program, or a doctor trying to get a Questioner to take a medication, or a spouse trying to get a Questioner's help in cleaning the basement, it's worth the effort to spell out the justifications: why this task, why this way, why now? If convinced—and that's a crucial *if*—the Questioners will reliably follow through.

The same process applies for Questioners considering an inner expectation. They'll meet an expectation for themselves once they're convinced it makes sense. Say a Questioner wants to get back in shape. That Questioner needs to take the time to do his research, weigh his options, and be convinced that a particular type of exercise, for him, is the most efficient and productive way to get fit. It doesn't matter if his doctor orders him to exercise, or his wife nags him, or his coworker says, "Let's be gym buddies"—but once the Questioner decides that CrossFit or running is the best form of exercise for him, he'll be able to meet his inner expectation.

Questioners question everything. One of my favorite examples of the Questioner Tendency in action came during a conference, when I asked the audience to divide into their Four Tendencies and create a motto for their Tendency. The four groups conferred, and when it was the Questioners' turn to present, they answered: "Why do we need a motto?" *Of course.*

Strengths (and Weaknesses)

Because Questioners are wholly inner-directed, once they make up their minds about the right course of action, they follow through without much difficulty—and they resist expectations without much difficulty, too. Questioners have the self-direction of Upholders, the reliability of Obligers, and the authenticity of Rebels.

Questioners may question even the most basic customs and assumptions. "Do I want to be married?" "If you're my boss, do I have to do what you tell me to do?" "Why shouldn't children be allowed to curse like adults?"

For Questioners, it's crucial that an expectation seem reasonable and justified. They resist rules for rules' sake. A Questioner wrote:

> I decide on a case-by-case basis what rules I'll follow. I take more than six items into the fitting room if no one's checking, because it's inconvenient to keep going in and out. I think the rule is in place not only to prevent theft (which I would never do), but to move things along if there's a line. Since I only shop during off hours, there never is a line, so I don't think the rule makes sense, hence, I don't follow it.

To a Questioner, this line of thinking is reasonable; a Rebel may get a kick out of breaking the rule, or at least feel indifferent to it. But an Upholder or an Obliger may think, "Why do you get to exempt yourself from a rule that everyone's expected to follow?"

Questioners almost never unquestioningly meet an expectation. A Questioner told me, "When I was going to join the Kappa Kappa Gamma sorority, they told me I'd have to vow to be 'womanly and true.' I thought, 'What does that even mean?' I burst out laughing and dropped out the next day."

Because Questioners require solid justifications for what they do, they can add tremendous value to relationships and organizations by ensuring that they—and also the people around them—don't unthinkingly accept expectations that aren't well justified. "Why do we bother to hold staff meetings? Why are we using this software? Why do we spend so much time chasing this client?"

In fact, Questioners are often puzzled by others' willingness to act without sound reasons. As one Questioner lamented, "I ask, 'Why do people do anything if they don't inwardly believe it's the right thing? What are we, a bunch of lemmings? On the other hand, if people really believe something is the right thing, why wouldn't they do it?'" (Note that this comment takes the form of three questions.)

Questioners want to make well-considered decisions and are often willing to do exhaustive research. They love to weigh their options. Just as Upholders love index cards, I've noticed that a love of spreadsheets is very common among Questioners—they also tend to send people lots of articles.

A Questioner wrote:

> For my master's degree, I've been indecisive about choosing a thesis topic. This semester, we have the option to do our assignments on our thesis topic, as a sort of prep for next year. Many classmates have written about their intended thesis topic all semester. I, however, have used this as an opportunity to try out a different topic on every single assignment. It has meant a lot of extra work, and now I know why. As a Questioner, I need to learn lots about a topic before I can commit.

Because of their enthusiastic research, Questioners often become resources for other people; they enjoy sharing their knowledge.

Along the same lines, Questioners tend to be very interested in improving processes. They like to eliminate mistakes and make things run better. A Questioner friend told me how much he'd enjoyed working as a fact-checker; another told me that his hobby was to work on user-interface improvements.

For Questioners, arguments like "We've always done it this way," or "This is standard practice," or "I'm the boss" carry no weight. They want to know *why*. Questioners will challenge assumptions, consider other alternatives, and reject conventional wisdom. One Questioner wrote:

> When I was younger, I didn't understand the point of fashion and makeup, so I ignored it. Now that I'm older and in the working world, it has been demonstrated to me (through both subjective experience and objective research) that one's appearance affects one's career track and interactions with others, and I put what I feel to be a reasonable amount of effort into looking attractive. I measure that against the amount of time I want to spend on inner work, since I believe that to be even more important.

A very Questioner way of thinking.

Questioners want to make up their own minds—even when given "expert" advice. They don't automatically accept authority, but always ask, "Why should I listen to this person, anyway?" For instance, before deciding to sign up for a class, they might interview the teacher, sit in on a few sessions, or ask for references.

"When I decided to lose weight," one Questioner recalled, "I made spreadsheets of the nutritionists, nutritional plans, and doctors I wanted to try, with their pros and cons. I found a nutritionist who met my requirements, and I'm mostly following her program."

As this comment illustrates, Questioners like to customize. One Questioner exhibited this Questioner desire—and also dislike of the arbitrariness of New Year's resolutions—when he told me, "I did a thirty-day workout video challenge, but I did it every other day instead of consecutive days. I happened to start it on January 1, and whenever I told anyone about it, I always emphasized that I just happened to start it on January 1—that it was not a New Year's resolution. At the time I didn't know that I'm a Questioner, but now I understand why it was so important to me to say that."

Weaknesses (and Strengths)

As with all of the Tendencies, the strengths of Questioners are also the weaknesses. As one Questioner explained, "While questioning has served me very well professionally—I'm a high-profile public company C-level executive, and a busy mother of young children—it's also absolutely exhausting. I question and requestion everyone and everything."

When Questioners don't accept the justification for an expectation, they refuse to meet it—which can get them into trouble. At home or at work, others may find their constant questioning to be tiresome, draining, or obstructive. Others may conclude that Questioners raise questions needlessly, or argue for the sake of arguing, or refuse to accept authority or decisions. For instance, one Questioner said, "When a new practice gets implemented at the company I work for, I'll often (quietly or loudly) boycott it until someone justifies the practice to my liking." To a Questioner, this seems sensible—but a manager or coworker might disagree.

A boss who doesn't understand a Questioner's ways may find the behavior annoying, or disrespectful, or decide that the Questioner "isn't a team player." One Questioner told me that he was fired because even though he was doing good work, his thin-skinned boss interpreted his barrage of questions as insubordination.

Similarly, for young Questioners, school can present a real challenge, because many school rules seem arbitrary or inefficient, and teachers and administrators often feel little obligation to justify them. In such a situation, Questioners may find it tough to complete necessary work, and they may act in ways that make them look uncooperative or impudent. One Questioner wrote:

> I've been showing my Questioner Tendency since I was a little girl, such as when I threw a fit over needing to send a Valentine Day's card to every kid in my class. In my eight-year-old mind, if I sent valentines to everyone, including the kids I didn't like, then the ones I sent to my real friends would be meaningless. Elementary school can be frustrating for us Questioners.

But the problem isn't limited to elementary school. Another Questioner explained:

> As a Questioner, I tend to question and disobey expectations I deem stupid, an inefficient use of my time, or arbitrary. As a graduate student, this has hindered me from completing coursework that I believe to be arbitrary—for example, weekly responses to prove that I've completed the readings. However, I gladly complete the challenging course deliverables such as projects and lab assignments, because I feel like I'm learning and being challenged.

The Questioners' constant questioning process may exhaust and drain the people around them, yet those questions must be answered if Questioners are to comply.

Questioners themselves sometimes wish they could stop questioning. "I always want to have just one more piece of information before I decide, and I can't ever stop." "I question outside rules too often. People often tell me, 'Give it a rest. Just get on with things!' I wish I could." All that questioning burns time and energy. In law school, a Questioner friend interviewed with dozens of law firms; I interviewed with six; we both ended up at the same firm.

The constant questioning means that Questioners sometimes suffer from *analysis-paralysis*. They want to continue to gather research, weigh their options, and consider more possibilities. They crave perfect information, but very often in life we must make decisions and move forward without perfect information.

Sometimes, too, questioning makes Questioners hesitate and stumble. For instance, many Questioners report that when they try to follow health advice, they begin to consider whether they're following the "best" approach—they think, "Maybe I should do more research, maybe there's a more efficient way, maybe this advice is incorrect," which stops their efforts.

In fact, because Questioners excel at looking for reasons and questioning decisions, if they want to find a rationale for avoiding an expectation or breaking a good habit, they can. They are good at identifying loopholes. As one Questioner explained:

> I can question and rationalize my way out of anything. My conversations in my head are often very Jekyll and Hyde: "You should exercise." "But it's too cold outside." "Do your

workout inside." "But I have too much work and that takes precedence over exercise!" I get overwhelmed by the internal dialogue, so I end up watching TV to turn off my brain.

Along those same lines, the Questioners' desire to customize, and their questioning of expert advice, can be frustrating for those to whom they turn for help, advice, or services: teachers, bosses, colleagues, doctors, college counselors, plumbers, lawn-care specialists. When I read about one survey in which 26% of doctors agreed with the statement "My patients think they know better than I do what's good for them," I thought, "Hmmm, sounds to me like they're Questioners." A Questioner explained: "I disregard 'expert' opinion often. My dentist suggests that patients get annual X-rays. I don't. I get them every five years, because I believe that frequent, unnecessary X-rays can be a cause of cancer."

Another Questioner summed up the Questioner perspective: "Any kind of medical person must hate to see me coming, because I always have a multitude of questions and won't leave until I'm satisfied. If I have some knowledge already, I may act on that, whether or not it concurs with medical advice. If I don't have the knowledge already, I take the answers to my questions and do my own research before deciding whether to follow advice."

As with all the Tendencies, a gift can become a curse. Because Questioners are motivated by sound reasons—or rather what they *believe* to be sound reasons, which sometimes aren't—they can sometimes seem like crackpots. They may reject the guidance of experts to follow their own conclusions and ignore those who argue, "Why do you think you know more about pneumonia than a trained doctor?" or "Everyone in the office uses one format for the reports, why do you insist on using your own crazy format?"

Judging from the material I read when I was writing my biography of John F. Kennedy, *Forty Ways to Look at JFK*, I suspect that many conspiracy theorists are Questioners.

In some situations, a Questioner's crackpot aspect may be tiresome. For instance, legendary entrepreneur and business leader Steve Jobs was a Questioner, and when he was a young man he believed that eating a fruit-heavy, vegetarian diet meant that he didn't need to worry about body odor— even though many people told him that, in fact, he *did* need to worry about it. And this aspect of the Questioner can actually become dangerous. When Jobs was first diagnosed with the cancer that led to his death, he rejected the accepted approach of chemotherapy and surgery, and unsuccessfully tried to cure himself using a self-prescribed regimen of acupuncture, a vegan diet, herbal remedies, and other nonconventional treatments before finally agreeing to surgery.

As with all the Tendencies, with wisdom and experience, Questioners can learn to manage the weaknesses of their Tendencies. One Questioner summarized: "As a Questioner, I've learned that I can get into trouble when I ignore rules without communicating. Now I follow the rules, change the rules—or move on."

One puzzling note about Questioners: They often remark on how much they hate to wait in line. A friend told me, "I hate waiting in line so much that I can't even carry on a conversation while waiting to be seated in a restaurant." Perhaps it's the inefficiency.

Variations Within the Tendency

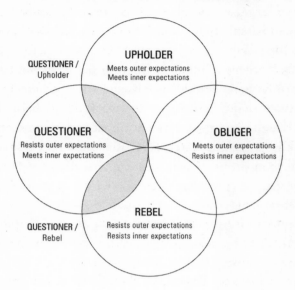

Like people of all Tendencies, Questioners can be very different from one another.

The Questioner Tendency overlaps with Upholder (both meet inner expectations) and Rebel (both resist outer expectations).

QUESTIONER/Upholders are more likely to meet outer expectations. They're fairly ready to accept the rationale for social expectations and general rules; one QUESTIONER/Upholder explained, "I have a deep belief that rules are probably there for a reason, even if I don't know what it is. It's important to me not to get in trouble and not to inconvenience others when I weigh my options. But if I don't think an activity has any useful purpose, I can't bring myself to do it."

My husband, Jamie, is a QUESTIONER/Upholder. He questions everything, but he can be persuaded fairly easily to meet an expectation. As an Upholder, I doubt I could be married happily to someone who wasn't like that. Which is a sobering thought.

On the other end of the spectrum, some Questioners tip toward Rebel; they challenge expectations so fiercely, and reject them so often, that they may look like Rebels. (The key differences? Questioners resist an expectation because they think it's unjustified; Rebels resist because they don't want to be controlled. Another telling distinction: If Questioners set an expectation for themselves, they have little trouble meeting it; Rebels struggle.)

Perhaps it's my Upholder nature, but I find it hilarious, and sometimes maddening, to hear Questioners-tipped-to-Rebels argue why they won't follow the rules.

For instance, some QUESTIONER/Rebels reject traffic regulations. One wrote, "I sneer at speed limits and drive what I feel comfortable with." When I wrote back to ask, "Do you think all drivers should drive at the speed that they think is safe?" the commenter replied, "Yes, it may be a good idea just to drive at whatever speed you are comfortable with. Most people have a certain speed they will not exceed, anyway. And you only have to travel the interstate to see just how much people abide by the speed limit, anyway. Like the drug laws, it is useless." That's the Questioner-tipped-to-Rebel perspective: The ineffectiveness and arbitrariness of a general expectation makes it illegitimate and therefore it should be disregarded.

Another QUESTIONER/Rebel wrote, "I received a ticket for parking the wrong way on the street; I have yet to pay it; I don't understand the purpose of how parking one

way or another keeps anyone safer, thus I'm not ponying up."
I fought back the impulse to respond, "Good luck with that."

The fact is, if Questioners disagree with an outer expectation, they feel entitled to dismiss it.

Depending on their personality, Questioners also vary in their decisiveness. Some Questioners suffer from analysis-paralysis. Their questioning, and their desire for more information, block them from moving forward. One Questioner explained, "I often find myself researching every brand, type, company, or offer before l will purchase something. I agonize over it, often for weeks at a time, before finally making a decision."

On the other hand, some Questioners are very decisive. My husband, Jamie, is a Questioner, and always wants to know why a certain thing should be done; but once his questions are answered, he acts fast.

Of course, many Questioners are a mix. One Questioner explained,

> I do occasionally fall into analysis-paralysis, but surprisingly this most often happens with seemingly unimportant decisions. I had no trouble deciding on a college major, whether or not to get married young, or whether or not to get a dog. However, I spent months deciding on what planner to order for the new year. My husband (Obliger) couldn't believe the amount of time I spent researching. When I finally hit the order button for a Day Designer, he was thrilled and said, "Can we stop discussing planners now?"

Another variation within the Questioner Tendency? Social adeptness. Socially skilled Questioners manage to pose their questions without annoying or draining others, or making them feel defensive. If Questioners find themselves accused of overquestioning, of lacking team spirit, or of being uncooperative, they may benefit from learning to pose questions differently. Instead of interrupting a boss's presentation to say abruptly, "This new rule doesn't make any sense," they can learn to ask, "Could you tell me why the rule was created? If I understand its purpose, I'll have a much easier time implementing it." Delivery can sometimes make a big difference in whether others see a Questioner as constructive or obstructive.

I've noticed another interesting pattern among Questioners: They often question the Four Tendencies framework itself.

Every time I give a talk about the Four Tendencies, I get a big laugh, and some nods of recognition, when I announce, "If your first reaction to the Four Tendencies is to think, 'Well, I question the validity of your framework,' you're probably a Questioner."

Partly this arises from their questioning nature, of course. Questioners qualify, hedge, and find exceptions to the answers they give on the quiz. They may also be skeptical about whether this framework has a sound basis in science or whether a single framework with four categories could describe all of humanity. Many Questioners have told me, "I question the validity of lumping all people into four broad categories."

"But here's the thing," I always answer. "Many people make that exact comment when I tell them about the Four Tendencies. They make the *very same objection* in practically identical words!" It's funny: their objection to categories puts them into a category.

But I believe that this skepticism also reflects the fact that the Questioner Tendency is the least *distinctive* Tendency. Upholders, Obligers, and Rebels recognize how they're different from other people. But Questioners view their questioning not as evidence of a pattern but as merely the logical, universal response to life. A friend told me, "I'm definitely a Questioner. Although doesn't everyone or at least most people think the same way?" Nope, they sure don't.

During a visit to my old high school, where I spoke about the Four Tendencies, a senior insisted, "I'm a mix of Tendencies. Sometimes I act one way, sometimes another, depending on the situation."

"For example?" I asked.

"If I get an assignment from a teacher I respect, I do it, no problem, so I'm an Upholder. But if I don't respect the teacher, I won't do it. So I'm a Rebel. So I'm different, depending on the situation."

"Actually, no," I said. "That's pure Questioner. A Questioner's first question is 'Why should I listen to you, anyway?'"

Why Questioners Dislike Being Questioned

There's a great irony lurking in the heart of the Questioner Tendency.

I knew that Questioners ask a lot of questions—but I was intrigued when a podcast listener asked, "Have you noticed that Questioners resist being questioned themselves?" I'd absolutely noticed it in my Questioner husband. In fact, his refusal to be questioned is so pronounced that in our family we have a long-running joke about "N2K." He provides answers on a "need to know" basis only. Whether it's "What are you making for dinner?" or "When will you start your new job?" Jamie refuses to answer. Which can drive me crazy.

I'd assumed this was just a provoking quirk of his personality. Instead, I now realize, it's an aspect of his Questioner Tendency. While Questioners usually don't mind providing information, many (though not all) Questioners object to being questioned about anything related to their judgment or decisions. And this can be a source of tension.

A Questioner wrote to explain:

> We Questioners are perpetually exasperated with people who, unlike us, haven't exhaustively researched the whys, pros, and cons of everything. If I've decided to go on a low-carb diet and some non-Questioner starts questioning me with "But I heard that those diets are really bad for your liver" or "But didn't Robert Atkins die young?" I get frustrated quickly. If these were valid concerns, obviously I would have discovered them—and then why would I be embarking on this diet? (Cue exasperation.)

Another Questioner agreed: "As a Questioner, I'd rather not explain myself, or why I'm doing something. We Questioners have thought about the logic behind our decision. So it's a) exhausting to revisit something and lay out all the reasons and/or b) we feel we're right, so we don't feel like we have to justify it to someone else."

Because Questioners make careful decisions, they're often annoyed—even insulted—when people question them. Which is funny, because people often feel that way about the questions of Questioners.

And, of course, Questioners particularly hate questions they consider a waste of their time. Their first question is "Why should I answer your question?" They're much more willing to answer a question if they understand why it's being asked. Not "What time are we leaving?" but "What time are we leaving? Because I'm wondering if I have time to go to the gym."

Not surprisingly, others get frustrated when Questioners refuse to answer questions. A Questioner explained, "Given how much effort I put into it, it's exasperating to have my deliberations ignored, dismissed, or . . . well . . . questioned." Understood. But other people need their questions answered, too.

So what to do? Instead of making Questioners feel that their decisions are being questioned, others can ask them to explain how they reached their conclusion. Questioners often enjoy teaching or sharing knowledge. For instance: "I'd love to know your thought process. It would help me to understand how you got to that decision." Or: "I was interested to see that you chose that reporting software, and I'd be curious to hear about why it's the best one."

How Questioners Can Master Analysis-Paralysis

The Questioner impulse to question can become draining and paralyzing, both for Questioners themselves and for the people around them. As discussed above, some Questioners struggle to end the research phase and move into action. One Questioner wrote: "I can't stop researching different approaches for various goals (diet, exercise, finances, work). I'm obsessed with finding the most efficient way—which is entirely inefficient. I'm distracted by every shiny new theory or approach."

For this reason, Questioners need to limit their overdeliberation. To avoid getting distracted by the urge to dig deeper, Questioners should focus on their ultimate aim. A Questioner friend told me, "I have an insatiable need for information, so when I feel myself getting sucked into research mode, I ask myself, 'Is this information actually relevant to what I'm trying to decide? Why am I spending this time and energy on this question?'"

"You question your own questioning!" I said.

Another Questioner told me, "When I work with private clients, my Questioner Tendency used to make it difficult for me to keep appointments within the allotted time, because I always wanted to know more and provide more information."

"So how did you change?" I asked, curious.

"I tapped deeper into my Questioner side and reminded myself of all the very good reasons that sticking to a schedule would be good for me and my clients."

Another approach? Questioners might choose to avoid situations that require a lot of research, analysis, and decision making. One Questioner wrote ruefully, "Designing and building a home—what was I thinking? I've spent hours upon hours online poring through product reviews and forums, figuring out which was the 'best' of everything from flooring to central vacuum systems. Which would be fine if I enjoyed doing it, but I don't." It would have been better for her to have hired a contractor she trusted to do this work.

Of course, finding an expert to "trust" is a challenge. But Questioners with analysis-paralysis can solve it by following the lead of someone they respect or restricting their information sources—checking *Consumer Reports;* finding the doctor, expert, or other authority they consider reliable; calling a respected friend or family member; or deciding that "the clerks at this camping store are really knowledgeable, so I'm going to buy a tent at this store, I'm not going to let myself go anywhere else."

Questioners who suffer from analysis-paralysis, or the people around them, can use deadlines to end research and force a decision—"We need an answer by Friday." But Questioners may question those limits! One Questioner wrote, "The advice to use a deadline is something I question itself. I only respond to deadlines that make sense. Arbitrary ones don't work."

But for Questioner overquestioning, or any kind of Questioner paralysis, the most important cure is *clarity*. Is a Questioner struggling to form a habit? Is a Questioner failing to meet an inner expectation? If so, the problem is often clarity—because when Questioners don't understand clearly *why* they should meet an expectation, and why they should meet it in a particular way, they won't meet it. Questioners need clarity, and to get clarity, they can ask questions. (And their questions may suggest why they're doing certain things others may disapprove of.)

Why should I bother to do this at all?

Why should I listen to you; what's your expertise or authority? *"Does this nutritionist have the proper credentials to tell me what to eat?"*

Why should I have to do this, why can't someone else take care of it? *"Can I have surgery instead of doing physical therapy?"*

Can I get more information?

Can I tweak this expectation to suit my individual needs? *"I'm experiencing side effects. I'll lower my dosage, no need to tell my doctor."*

Is there a better way to do this? *"If I take all my pills in the morning, I get it over with at one time."*

Is this approach serving its purpose? *"I don't see why I should bother to take this medication if it doesn't make me feel better."*

Who benefits? What's the real intention of the person or organization setting this expectation? *"The doctor makes more money if I have this procedure every week."*

Once Questioners achieve clarity, they're able to act. One Questioner wrote:

> Knowing that I'm a Questioner allowed me to quit sugar. I couldn't do it when it was just a vague notion that sugar was bad for me. I needed research. So I watched lectures, scoured web articles, and read Gary Taubes's *Why We Get Fat*. Since then, I've found it relatively easy to cut sugar entirely. I needed clear, hard facts, and once I got them, changing my habit became much easier.

Note, however, that a Questioner's clarity may not result in the behavior that others are trying to promote.

How Questioners Can Meet Unjustified Expectations by Finding Their Own Justification

Questioners often run into trouble when they find themselves in a situation where it's important to meet an expectation—but they deem that expectation to be arbitrary, inefficient, or unjustified.

In such situations, Questioners can remind themselves that it may make sense to comply with an expectation—even a senseless or arbitrary one—because it's important to someone else, or because it's in their own self-interest.

One Questioner recalled:

> It took me a long time to realize that making my grandmother happy was a good enough reason, sometimes, to do what she asked. As a young adult, I drove her crazy with questioning what she wanted me to do. Why dry the dishes when they can drain in the dish rack perfectly well? Why can't I wear all black all the time? But now I just think, "Well, I'll do these pointless things because they actually do have a point, which is to please my grandmother."

A worried-looking medical student asked me, "How do I make myself do something when I'm asked to do something arbitrary or just purely stupid? This happens practically every day, and it's very hard for me to handle."

"Right," I said, nodding. "This comes up often with Questioners."

"So what do I do?"

"Don't just focus on the first order of reason, but think about the second order of reason. You're doing it for your reasons. 'Yes, this assignment is pointless, and it bugs me to waste time, but I want to earn my professor's respect. My own goal justifies doing it his way.'"

As these examples illustrate, even when the first order of justification is missing—"Does this expectation make sense on its own?"— Questioners can focus on the second order of justification—"Does it make sense for me to meet this otherwise unjustified expectation, for my own reasons?" It's important for Questioners to remind themselves to do what they *must* so that they can do what they *want*.

SUMMARY: QUESTIONER

LIKELY STRENGTHS:

Data-driven

Fair-minded (according to his or her judgment)

Interested in creating systems that are efficient and effective

Willing to play devil's advocate

Comfortable bucking the system if it's warranted

Inner-directed

Unwilling to accept authority without justification

POSSIBLE WEAKNESSES:

Can suffer analysis-paralysis

Impatient with what he or she sees as others' complacency

Crackpot potential

Unable to accept closure on matters that others consider settled
if questions remain unanswered

May refuse to observe expectations that others find fair or at least
nonoptional (e.g., traffic regulations)

May resist answering others' questions

6

Dealing with a Questioner

"Why do we need a motto?"

Work • Spouse • Child • Health Client • Choosing a
Career

Dealing with a Questioner at Work

Questioners can be very valuable for organizations, because
they're the ones asking questions like "Why should we do it
this way? Should we be doing it at all? Should we interview
more people? Is there a better way to structure this?"

Questioners love research, finding efficiencies, and elimi-
nating irrational processes. They reject lazy explanations like
"This is the way we've always done it." Their questioning ensures that an organization uses its resources most effectively.

However, even though it's often valuable to the team effort, the Questioner's relentless questioning isn't always appreciated by coworkers and bosses. One Questioner explained:

Being a Questioner helps me perform the core work of my
job well. However, sometimes, when people are willing to

go with the flow on a collaborative team project, they view my need to ask questions as not showing team spirit. I think that by politely asking questions (even "Do we really need to do this project?"), we often can clarify our approach, prevent false steps and needless work, and end up with a better result. My zeal for saving time, money, and effort is often appreciated, but it also can annoy people who take any question as criticism or respond with "Because so-and-so says so" or "Because it's always been this way." These answers are possibly the two most infuriating justifications anyone could present to a Questioner.

When Questioners refuse to follow an accepted practice, burn up time questioning issues that others considered settled, or can't make a decision in a timely way, they can seem difficult. Coworkers can help them avoid overquestioning by putting limits on their investigations. For instance, a manager might tell a Questioner who's interviewing people for a new hire to decide by a certain date or to consider only the top five candidates. Limitation helps force action.

Because Questioners have great faith in their own analysis and judgment, they can become convinced of the rightness of their own views and refuse to be persuaded otherwise.

The head of a firm told me, "My v-p for research is brilliant, but I can't stand working with him. He questions my decisions and my judgment nonstop. My authority and my expertise mean nothing to him."

I said, "He probably doesn't mean to be undermining. He just questions everything, it's his nature."

"Well, whatever the reason, we can't even have a conversation anymore. I have to deal with him through an intermediary."

When coworkers realize that the Questioner doesn't intend to be confrontational, or uncooperative, or obstructionist, but is just acting according to his or her Tendency, they find it much easier to be patient and to provide the information that the Questioner needs. One Obliger reported, "I'm a Montessori teacher and I work closely with two Questioners. I used to be infuriated by them daily, but now I suggest books, websites, or articles they can consult to answer their questions."

When Questioners work for themselves—start their own business or generate their own type of work—they do well at any task they've decided is worth their time and energy. They're committed to doing only the things that make sense—which, as always, is both a help and a hindrance. For instance, Questioners might not want to waste time in small talk with potential clients—unless they conclude that it will help to close the deal.

Questioners may also need to take steps to deal with analysis-paralysis, because going solo requires many complex decisions: What's the best way to keep records, file taxes, get health insurance, handle marketing? A Questioner working alone may become frozen with indecision.

Dealing with a Questioner Spouse

A Questioner wrote, "I'm a Questioner and I'm always asking why and how things can be better. My wife jokes that she knows we're married forever, because I already did the research and made the decision. She's actually right!"

I have a lot of exposure to the Questioner Tendency, because my husband, Jamie, is a Questioner. Being married to a Questioner is often helpful to me because as an Upholder, my instinct is to meet an expectation without questioning it closely. Sometimes I imagine expectations where none exist, or I become too concerned with sticking to the rules. But Jamie always questions an expectation before he'll comply with it, and seeing his example has taught me to question more.

However, while I respect and often strive to emulate this aspect of Jamie's character, sometimes it drives me nuts. I'd prefer a spirit of ready cooperation in our household, but now I understand that he's not trying to be obstructionist, he just wants to know why he should do what I ask.

Recently, I wanted Jamie to pick up some deli turkey on his way home from the gym. Jamie doesn't like that job, because he doesn't like to wait in line while they slice the meat (Questioners hate to wait in line). Before I knew he was a Questioner, I might have texted him, "Pls pick up shaved smoked turkey on yr way home." And, I'm confident, he would've ignored my request. Not because he's a jerk, but because he would've reasoned, "Why should I have to do this chore? Why buy turkey when we have plenty of food at home? It's not a good use of my time." Keeping his Questioner Tendency in mind, I wrote, "Pls pick up turkey on yr way home. Eleanor has 2 field trips this week so we need to pack lunch." He bought the turkey.

At times a Questioner's questions can make a spouse feel under attack or unsupported. One Questioner wrote:

> I always need to understand why, and this has been a big strain on my marriage. My husband feels disrespected by the explanation he has to give to ask me for a simple favor. "Honey, would you buy a new lightbulb?" has turned into a two-day fight. I'll be damned if I'm going to buy the lightbulb without understanding all the details.

A Questioner friend is married to an Upholder. "My husband hates to see drawers and cabinets open in the kitchen," she recounted. "So he said to me, 'Let's have a rule that we always close the kitchen cabinets and drawers.'"

I nodded. "Right. To an Upholder, once something's a rule, it gets done."

"But I said, 'Why do you get to make a rule?' and he said, 'I'll make this rule, you make another rule.' And I told him, 'I don't want to make rules for you or have you follow my rules. Why should we do that? Why do the drawers and cabinets have to be closed, anyway? If you want them closed, you can close them. But it doesn't bug me, so why should I bother?'"

I started to laugh. "You're such a Questioner and he's such an Upholder! Classic." I love to see the Tendencies play out right in front of me.

Because Questioners put such great weight on their own analysis, they often resist the advice of "experts"—which can be frustrating for spouses. One reader wrote, "My Questioner husband thinks he knows the answers to everything, and in fact, he's often right, which makes it even harder. Example: I want to go to a financial adviser. He thinks it's a waste of money, he feels that he can just research everything and know as much as anyone else." This pattern can be annoying, but it can also be downright life-threatening—say, if a Questioner decides that a power tool's safety features aren't actually necessary.

The Questioner drive for information and desire to make the best decision can trap a couple in analysis-paralysis. One reader wrote:

Because my husband is a Questioner, nothing seems to get done. For example, I found a preschool I think would work for our child, but my husband questions the decision. In another case, we need to have concrete steps made, but he questions the contractor's plan for the steps. I'm trying to get things done, and he puts up a yellow signal with so many questions that I just give up.

She might consider strategies used to help Questioners escape analysis-paralysis, such as setting action deadlines, following the advice of a respected adviser, or limiting information sources.

As with all the Tendencies, the upside of the Questioner Tendency is the same as the downside. And spouses experience both.

Dealing with a Questioner Child

To a Questioner child, "Because I say so," "We've always done it this way," "This is what you have to do," and "That's the rule" are infuriating justifications and certainly don't warrant compliance.

A Questioner needs reasons. If a parent wants a Questioner child to practice the piano, it would be important to address his or her questions, such as: Why play the piano at all? Why is it important to practice? Why practice a certain number of days? Why this particular teacher? If music is important, why not just listen, why play? If a Questioner child is satisfied with these explanations, he or she is much more likely to practice regularly. A child who isn't satisfied, however, may resist mightily.

Parents and teachers may become annoyed when Questioner children refuse to follow conventional behavior. They ask, "Why can't I wear my Halloween costume to school?" "Uncle Jimmy is rude to me, so why do I have to be polite to him?" "What's the point of college?" One reader wrote, "My teen son is a Questioner. He just got his driver's license, and he was driving barefoot after a swim meet. I said, 'Put on shoes, it's illegal to drive barefoot' (I'm an Upholder), and he said, 'But why is it illegal?'" (Some Questioners really take issue with traffic regulations.)

Teachers and professors may be enthusiastic about a Questioner's probing questions because it pushes class discussion forward and shows a student's engagement. Or they may become exasperated, if in their judgment, the Questioner slows down discussion too much, challenges their authority, argues against or refuses to complete assignments, or misdirects the energy of the class.

Childhood can be a painful time for Questioners, because children are so often expected to do things because an adult "said so." A parent of a Questioner child told me, "My son is very intelligent, but he does badly in school. He aces the exams, but he doesn't see the point of homework, so he refuses to do it."

Questioners' frustrations with school can have a significant effect on their academic success; when dealing with a child who refuses to meet an expectation, it's important to try to understand the reason for that child's behavior. While a Rebel child might think, "You can't make me," a Questioner child may be waiting to hear a convincing argument about why meeting an expectation is worthwhile. One Questioner recalled:

> When I was a little kid, my handwriting was very messy, and my teachers seemed more concerned with that than the

content of my work. I was a smart kid, and one day I realized that I knew the answers to all the questions in the textbooks, and there was no reason why I should have to write anything down. If the teachers wanted to know my answers, they should ask me, and I would tell them!

Teachers would punish me, they called me lazy, stubborn, and slow, but they didn't give me a good counter-argument. It was only when the work got complicated enough that I had to write down my work or lose the thread of my thoughts that I started writing.

If a teacher had bothered to find out the reason for this child's refusal and provided adequate explanations, that school conflict might have been vanquished much earlier.

The fact is, Questioner children often clash with authority. I'm always pleased to see examples of the Four Tendencies—whether in real life or in books, movies, or television shows—and when I was re-reading Charlotte Brontë's *Jane Eyre*, I saw that *on the very first page of the book*, Jane's hateful aunt Mrs. Reed literally calls her a "Questioner" to explain why she finds Jane annoying: "Jane, I don't like cavillers or questioners." (I had to look up "caviller"; it means "one who quibbles.")

So when a Questioner child questions an assignment or expectation, a teacher or parent would do well to provide a thoughtful justification. If a Questioner student asks, "Why do I need to know about ancient Mesopotamia? This will never be of any use to me," a teacher might respond unhelpfully, "This is what we're studying now, so get with the program," or helpfully, "You're learning about Mesopotamia, true, but this assignment is teaching you much more. You're learning how to analyze complex material quickly, how to pull essential ideas out of a text, how to take notes efficiently, and how to explain ideas in your own words. These are important skills that will serve you well."

Beyond that, even children can respond to the "second order of reason." Why not drive barefoot? Because if you do, you may have to pay a big fine or have your license suspended. Why take courses that seem pointless? Because we can't afford to pay for college, and these courses are necessary if you're going to qualify for financial aid. Why be nice to Uncle Jimmy? Because you love Grandpa, and he'll be upset if you're rude to your uncle.

Dealing with a Questioner Patient or Health Client

For any health-care professional, it's crucial (although sometimes not possible) to answer the Questioner's questions. Once Questioners are convinced, they have little trouble meeting health expectations. They'll take medication, do physical therapy, change their eating and drinking habits, or show up for checkups. But if they're not convinced, they won't.

Too often, health-care professionals believe they've provided strong justifications for their expectations—but they've left questions unanswered, so the Questioner won't act. For instance, a dental hygienist might say, "You need to brush for two minutes, at least twice a day, or tartar will build up." That sounds like a justification. But what is tartar, anyway? What are the consequences of tartar buildup? And even if tartar is a problem, why not just wait for the dental hygienist to scrape it off? A little more explanation might lead to much better adherence.

It's worth noting, too, that Questioners often show a strong urge to customize. They may decide to follow instructions in the way they think makes the most sense—i.e., not exactly as prescribed. For that reason, it's important to explain why instructions should be followed precisely: "This medication should be taken at mealtimes, because otherwise it can cause severe nausea."

Questioners need reasons. Why cut back on carbs? Why walk up and down the aisle of an airplane? And do they fully trust the authority directing them to do such things? If so, they'll do it. If not, they won't. Questioners will do what they think makes sense, as customized for them. A Questioner friend reported:

> When I was diagnosed with type 2 diabetes, my girlfriend thought it would be hard for me to deal with my new eating plan—but I knew I could do it. When we were in the doctor's office, though, she thought I was out of hand, because I was asking so many questions. I knew that I needed the facts. Once I make up my mind, I stick with it. But I was honest with my doctor. I told him, "Fact is, I'm going to eat right, but I'm going to have six beers a week. And that's the way I'm going to do it."

The Questioner "crackpot" aspect (it's a harsh word, but there's no better term for the convinced-of-one's-own-nonexpert conclusions) is often seen in relation to health—perhaps it's the combination of the ability to do extensive research, often on unreliable Internet sites, along with the Questioner desire to customize.

Questioners may come up with their own theory about the cause of a health problem or what the treatment should be. In my observation, health professionals often ignore these patient-generated theories and just keep repeating their own view of the case, with the expectation that the patient will eventually accept the expert opinion. This approach often doesn't work. It's far more effective to address the patient's theory and explain why the professional doesn't agree with it.

A friend's Questioner husband took charge of his own cancer treatment—much to the dismay of his wife and doctors. They kept asking, "Why do you think you know more than a team of cancer doctors?" But he'd done his own research and drawn his own conclusions, and that carried more weight to him than any expert authority. To persuade him otherwise, the people around him would've done better to scrutinize the facts and reasoning that he found compelling and to present their facts and reasoning behind a different medical recommendation rather than just repeating, "Can't you listen to the doctors?"

In the health-care area (or any other area), when encouraging Questioners to take action, it can be useful to remind them, "Just try it. It's an experiment. If it works, keep going. If it doesn't, try something else." This approach appeals to the Questioner desire to gather information and to customize. Or Questioners might also follow the example of someone they respect as a role model: "If that approach works well for him, it might work well for me."

Choosing a Career as a Questioner

People often say things like, "I'm a journalist, so of course I must be a Questioner," or "Questioners are probably more likely to become scientists." But it doesn't work like that.

Most jobs could be filled by all of the Tendencies, because so many factors contribute to success in a particular career. After all, the Tendency describes only how a person responds to an expectation, not what the person's talents, personality, intelligence, or interests are. I have a friend who is a brilliant, highly analytical doctor. She loves research, she asks a lot of questions—and she's an Obliger. Because when it comes to meeting expectations, she readily meets outer expectations but struggles to meet inner ones.

That said, Questioners do tend to delight in information and analysis, so they thrive in environments that emphasize research. They enjoy improving systems. One Questioner explained:

> I'm an internal auditor for a large multinational corporation, and I've spent twenty years asking why the company does things the way it does and constantly looking for ways to improve methods. I'm well respected because I always take the time to explain why I recommend doing things a certain way, while remaining open to others' ideas. I doubt I would have been so successful in my job if I were any other Tendency.

Many professions benefit from the Questioner emphasis on reason and explanation. One Questioner explained:

> I'm a Questioner who tips toward Upholder. I work as a land-use planner for a small municipality, dealing mostly with new developments. Part of this is ensuring that development proposals follow the city rules (i.e., the building is x big, and y tall, and z far away from the street, etc.). But a lot of it can be based on discretion and interpretation.

My Tendency makes dealing with developers easier—I only make them do the things that make practical sense for the site, and I can explain why they should spend their money in this way. But my Upholder colleague clings to the rules, whether or not they're applicable, and often ends up in conflicts with the developers, our managers, and the municipal council.

Questioners do well in an environment that encourages and rewards questioning and where they're working with people who have a high tolerance for being questioned. Questioners don't work well with people who make arguments like "Because I said so" or "We've always done it this way."

When possible, Questioners should steer clear of bosses and colleagues who interpret constant questioning as undermining, uncooperative, or obstructive. One Questioner recalled, "I worked for a boss who wanted everyone to be a 'team player.' I consider myself a team player, and part of my value to the team is to help make sure we're doing our best work in the best way. But whenever I asked questions, he'd view it as me resisting being a team player."

Because Questioners need to understand why they're doing what they're doing, some want to be their own bosses, where they can do their own research and make their own decisions.

Questioners hate doing anything arbitrary or irrational or inefficient, so whatever career they follow, they'd be wise to avoid those conditions. Questioners who overdeliberate may do better when they work in a place where deadlines force action or where they have managers or coworkers who can help them set reasonable boundaries on their research.

SUMMARY: DEALING WITH
A QUESTIONER

They question all expectations and meet them only
if they believe they're justified, with the result that they
may meet only inner expectations

They put a high value on reason, research, and information

They make decisions based on information and reason;
sometimes, the reason is that it's important to someone else

They follow the advice of "authorities" only if they
trust their expertise

They follow their own judgment—sometimes even when it
flies in the face of experts who (allegedly) know more

They persistently ask questions, which may make them
seem uncooperative or defiant

They hate anything arbitrary—rules like "Five garments
to a fitting room"

They dislike being questioned themselves; they consider
their actions carefully so they find it tiresome or even
insulting to be asked to justify their decisions

They may have trouble delegating decision making, because
they suspect that others don't have a sufficient basis for
action

OBLIGER

"You can count on me, and I'm counting on you to count on me"

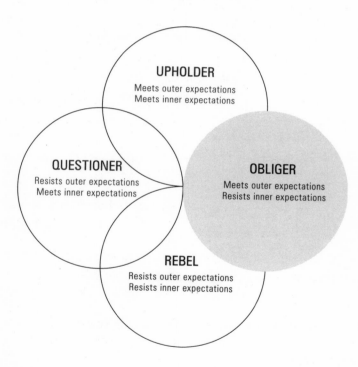

UPHOLDER
Meets outer expectations
Meets inner expectations

QUESTIONER
Resists outer expectations
Meets inner expectations

OBLIGER
Meets outer expectations
Resists inner expectations

REBEL
Resists outer expectations
Resists inner expectations

"You can count on me, and I'm counting on you to count on me."

"BY SERVING OTHERS, I SERVE MYSELF."

"If I have to, I will; if I want to, I won't."

"I'll do anything you ask. Until I won't."

"We need an outside commitment for everything—even to spend time with ourselves."

"SAY YES TO LESS."

"I have a long wick with a quick burn."

"Treat yourself as you treat others."

"How can I be of service to you?"

"I don't want to, but I will, anyway."

"All for one, and one for all."

7

Understanding the Obliger

"I'll do anything you ask. Until I won't."

Strengths (and Weaknesses) • Weaknesses (and Strengths) • Variations Within the Tendency • How Obligers Can Meet Inner Expectations by Creating Outer Accountability • When Outer Accountability Disappears • How Obligers Can Manage the Pros and Cons of the Tendency • How Obligers Shift the Line Between Outer and Inner Expectations • How to Understand and Protect Against Obliger-Rebellion

As we move through our days, we confront a barrage of expectations—the *outer* expectations that others impose (or try to impose) on us and the *inner* expectations that we impose (or try to impose) on ourselves.

Obligers readily meet the *outer* expectations imposed by others but struggle to meet the *inner* expectations they want to impose on themselves. Identifying the Obliger Tendency finally gave me the answer to my friend who asked, "I never missed practice when I was on the high school track team, so why can't I make myself go running now?" When my friend had a coach and a team counting on her—external expectations—she had no trouble showing up for practice, but her own inner expectation wasn't enough to get her running.

As a result, Obligers respond to external accountability. They wake up and think, "What must I do today? For whom?" When an expectation comes from the outside—from a boss, a client, a family member, a doctor, a coach, an accountability group, a colleague—Obligers will respond. For the most part, they meet deadlines, they keep their promises, they follow through for others.

However, Obligers struggle to follow through for *themselves*. For Obligers, it's the *inner* expectations that pose the challenge. No matter how much they may want to meet a purely inner expectation—to exercise, to take an online course, to start their own company—they will almost inevitably fail. That's a harsh thing to recognize, but it's true.

The good news is that this Obliger pattern is easily remedied—once an Obliger knows how to do it.

And how *does* an Obliger meet an inner expectation? *By creating outer accountability.* Once Obligers realize that outer accountability is the crucial missing element, the solution is very straightforward and easy to supply.

For this reason, Obligers are the ones who gain the most from learning about their Tendency. Even more than for Upholders, Questioners, and Rebels, the Four Tendencies framework helps Obligers analyze their behavior and shows them how to make desired changes. (And it also helps people around Obligers understand how to influence them effectively.)

This matters, because of all the Tendencies, the Obliger Tendency is the largest Tendency, for both men and women.

Strengths (and Weaknesses)

The Obliger is the rock of the world. At work, at home, and in life, not only are Obligers the biggest group, they're the ones whom people count on the most. Obligers show up, they answer the midnight call from the client, they meet their deadlines, they fulfill their responsibilities, they volunteer, they help out (until they stop—see the discussion later on Obliger-rebellion). Whether at work or at home, Obliger is the Tendency that's most likely to contribute.

I was preparing to speak at a conference on the Four Tendencies, and although I usually don't use slides, the conference organizer urged me to include them in my talk.

"I don't know how to create slides," I admitted.

"Oh, send me the text, and I'll create them," the organizer said.

"Hmmmmm . . ." I said, clearly conveying my doubts about whether that would actually happen.

"I'm an Obliger," he added.

"Oh," I answered, "in that case, thank you, can I have them by Friday?"

"Sure," he said, and we both laughed.

Obligers excel at meeting other people's demands and deadlines. Because of their active sense of obligation to others, they make great leaders, team members, friends, family members. The Obliger is the mainstay of every community. They will often say, "I put my patients/clients/research team/family ahead of myself."

Also, it's appropriate that the term "Obliger" begins with the letter "O," because just as blood type O is the universal blood type, the O Tendency is the universal partner; Obligers get along most easily with the other three Tendencies.

When Obligers have the external accountability they need to meet their inner expectations, they don't experience any sense of limitation or self-frustration—and of course many environments, such as the workplace, tend to supply lots of accountability. When what others expect from Obligers is what they expect from themselves, they have the life they want.

My mother is a great example of this. She's an Obliger, but partly by her design and partly probably by chance, she always finds external accountability to meet important aims for herself. For years, she got herself to exercise regularly by walking with a friend who lived next door. She loves to read, and she's in a book group. Obligers like my mother aren't frustrated by the difficulty they face in meeting inner expectations—they might never even *notice* this difficulty—because the fabric of their lives allows them to do so without much fuss.

Weaknesses (and Strengths)

For Obligers, no matter how much they may want to meet their inner expectations, if they don't have some kind of outer accountability, that expectation won't be met. In the representative sample I studied, more than two-thirds of Obligers answered that they were most likely to be frustrated with themselves because they feel like "I can take time for other people, but I can't take time for myself."

For this reason, Obligers struggle to self-motivate—to work on a Ph.D. thesis or a spec script, to attend networking events, to get their car serviced, even to get a massage. This can be a serious problem. An Obliger who dreams of launching a start-up, or of switching careers midstream, or of giving up fast food may feel very frustrated by his or her inability to follow through on these aims. An Obliger summarized: "Promises made to yourself can be broken. It's the promises made to others that should never be broken."

Obligers depend on outer accountability to meet both their outer and inner expectations; if that accountability is missing, they struggle.

At the same time, however, if the burden of outer expectations becomes too heavy, Obligers may show "Obliger-rebellion": they meet, meet, meet an expectation, then suddenly they snap and refuse to meet that expectation any longer. Acts of Obliger-rebellion can be small and symbolic or large and destructive.

Obligers need outer accountability to meet expectations, but they also need to guard against allowing those expectations to trigger Obliger-rebellion.

Variations Within the Tendency

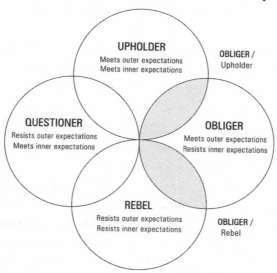

All Obligers respond to external expectations, but they vary *tremendously* in how and when they respond to them.

Like the other Tendencies, Obliger overlaps with two Tendencies: with Upholder (both meet outer expectations) and Rebel (both resist inner expectations).

While it might seem that OBLIGER/Upholders would feel more pressure to meet all expectations, and therefore experience more resentment and burnout, in fact, the opposite is true. Obliger-tipped-to-Upholders tend to have a clearer sense of their own capacities and desires and a greater ability to say no, just as Upholders can say no.

My sister, Elizabeth, is an OBLIGER/Upholder. She's an Obliger who readily meets outer expectations and struggles to meet inner expectations; nevertheless, at a certain point, she's able to say, "Nope, sorry, I can't do that." She hates to let people down, but if she knows that she won't be able to meet an expectation, she can say no without too much trouble. She finds it fairly easy to tell herself, "To say yes to you, I have to say no to someone else, so sorry, can't do that." Neither she nor I could remember many examples of her showing Obliger-rebellion. (Though a few do come to mind—for instance, the time she made a special stop at a Walgreens, bought a bag of potato chips, and ate them in the parking lot. "I'd never done anything like that before," she said. "It felt illegal.")

By contrast, OBLIGER/Rebels chafe more under external expectations and feel more resentful about others' demands. Like Rebels, they often feel pushed around, and they find it hard to count on themselves, and they react against any sense of coercion. Their Obligerness means that they find it hard to say no, but then they're likely to feel resentful and burned out and therefore more likely to show Obliger-rebellion. They meet expectations, but at a certain point (and they may reach that point very quickly), they snap. Like Rebels, they may dislike living with routines, a set calendar, and structure. As one OBLIGER/Rebel explained:

> I feel huge pressure to comply with other people's expectations, while seething with resentment internally. I find this particularly exhausting at work—I inwardly rebel every time I get an email asking me to do something or sit down to plan a project, but still feel obliged to get the work done. I know external accountability will help me establish the habits I want, but the idea of creating external accountability systems can make my skin crawl. I hate being told what to do.

Also, some Obligers describe themselves as "people-pleasers," but Obligers have a wide range of ideas about what they feel "obliged" to do. Some feel obliged to do a lot; some feel obliged to do very little. Is a person obliged to send handwritten thank-you notes? To stay late when the team's monthly report is due? To volunteer for the assignment that no one else is willing to tackle? Some Obligers will feel obliged to do it; other Obligers won't.

For some Obligers, expectations attach very easily. Like the Obliger who wrote to me, "Gosh, you know you're an Obliger when your first thought is: 'Take the Four Tendencies Quiz; you ought to help Gretchen with her research.'"

In fact, for some Obligers, expectations attach so easily that they feel obliged to do things that no one is actually expecting from them. "Everyone expects me to make slides for the meeting." (Really?) "It's totally unacceptable to have dirty dishes in the sink overnight." (Unacceptable to whom?) "Everyone's counting on me to organize a conference." (Are they counting on that? Even if they are, so what?)

These Obligers may feel enormous pressure to meet external obligations that, ironically, they've imposed on themselves. Even though such expectations are self-generated, they nevertheless take their force from the outside. As one Obliger put it:

> As I grow to believe others expect something of me, I'm more likely to do it. Examples: I gathered the trash a few times before garbage day when my husband was late at work, and now it's become my thing ... not because my husband expects it, but because I believe he does. Even though I know that he doesn't! Same thing with yoga class ... I forced myself to go a few times, and now I can't skip, because I'd disappoint the instructor.

She's not doing these activities because she wants to do them; she feels obliged to others, even though they aren't actually imposing an expectation.

By contrast, other Obligers feel *much less* sense of obligation. These Obligers don't struggle much with the burden of expectations or "people-pleasing." If no penalty is in place, they don't worry about meeting an expectation.

Also, Obligers vary in their energy levels. High-energy Obligers more easily meet expectations, while low-energy Obligers may feel burned out more quickly.

How Obligers Can Meet Inner Expectations by Creating Outer Accountability

So what can Obligers do to get themselves to meet an inner expectation? It's simple and easy—at least in theory.

To meet inner expectations, *Obligers must create structures of outer accountability*. They need tools such as supervision, late fees, deadlines, monitoring, and consequences enforced from the outside to keep their promises to themselves. For Obligers, this is the *crucial* element. Obligers (and the people around Obligers) can't expect that they'll be motivated by inner motivation or that they'll be convinced by consequences; they must have outer accountability.

Once Obligers recognize their need for outer accountability, they can build it in. One reader explained:

> I've struggled with setting good routines for myself, but I'll often spend a weekend watching my sister's five kids or my brother's six kids so the couples can get away for a few days—and every time I snap into this automatic routine for sleep, meals, church. I began to wonder: Why does taking care of these kids make me so much better at habits?
>
> I'd found the same thing as a young adult. When I was twenty-one, I served an eighteen-month mission for my church (LDS), and a unique aspect of a mission is that you spend 24/7 with a companion. You must remain in eyesight of that companion at all times. We had a strict schedule as missionaries of arising, having personal and companionship study or devotionals, exercising, getting ready, and working from 9:30 a.m. to 9:30 p.m. I thrived in that atmosphere.

A companionship was an automatic relationship, and we were expected to do the same thing at the same time together every day, so it was built-in accountability and monitoring.

There, I had good habits of sleeping, eating, spiritual devotion, exercise, work. But I couldn't maintain them once I came home. I often wished I could return to having a full-time companion where we were working on the same thing, at the same time, with the same goals.

Last week I had company, and I was up early, making meals, doing household tasks. My guests left this morning, and I was in my kitchen admiring how clean it was, despite all of my hours of cooking the last few days. Then I made lunch, and I didn't clean up after myself, and I caught myself thinking, "No one's here, it's just me." So I played a mental game with myself and pretended that some nieces and nephews were coming over later, and that got me to clean the kitchen.

The secret to success? Obligers must pick the right kind of accountability for them. Obligers vary *dramatically* in what makes them feel accountable.

Some Obligers are easily made to feel accountable. An auto-generated email, or an app that highlights an unfinished task on a to-do list, or a buzzing Fitbit, might be enough.

By contrast, some Obligers feel accountable only to an actual person. As one Obliger wrote: "I told everyone that I'm sugar-free, and it has been easy to avoid it when anyone is around. The only failure I've had was one afternoon when I was unexpectedly alone in the house." For an Upholder, Questioner, or Rebel, it wouldn't have mattered that no one else was home, but for this Obliger, it was a crucial element of the situation.

One Obliger analyzed how different methods did and didn't work for him:

> Knowing that external accountability is key for me, I made the switch from "working out" at home (almost never) to joining QiFlow fitness. Because of demand, my gym asks members to sign up online, and if you cancel less than two hours before a class, you're charged with a $5 "late cancel" fee. Strangely, it's less the $5 fee that keeps me from cancelling, but rather that I don't want an empty space in a class that I should've filled.

In fact, I've been struck by the fact that for many Obligers, the prospect of wasting money doesn't bring a sense of accountability. An Obliger friend told me, "I've always wanted to try yoga, and I've been trying to get myself to take a class for years. Finally, I actually signed up—and I went one time. It was the $300 yoga class." Maybe, for some Obligers, money doesn't provide accountability because it's their own money; if they're wasting someone else's money, they might feel accountable.

To be sure, some Obligers are able to manufacture a feeling of "external" accountability themselves, by creating external systems—to-do lists, calendar items, reminders on their phone—that provide that sense of external accountability, even though they're self-generated. From the outside, these Obligers look like Upholders, because they appear to be following an inner expectation. But for the Obliger, the expectation feels imposed from the outside.

Some imaginative Obligers can even create outer accountability by thinking of themselves in the third person. "I don't feel a lot of obligation to do things for myself right now," one

Obliger told me, "but I do feel guilty if I don't meet future-me's needs. I hate going to the gym, but future-me will wish I'd stuck to my workout schedule—even though current-me hates it."

However, most Obligers can't self-generate outer accountability; they must find true external sources. They need accountability to feel *real*. As one Obliger put it:

> I respond poorly to "gimmicky" accountability. If someone is holding me accountable as a way of doing me a favor and helping me to achieve a goal, I know I have no real obligation to that person. When I was working on my doctoral dissertation, I had frequent check-ins with my thesis adviser—but never had much progress to show. We both knew I was behind, and my adviser was disappointed, but I knew that my lack of progress didn't matter to her career. There were no consequences for her, just for me. In the end, the only thing that helped was to find another person in the same program who was struggling with the same procrastination problem. We'd hold each other accountable—and I knew that if I dropped the ball or didn't show up, then my partner would lose the feeling of accountability and stop working, too.

Other variations? Some Obligers—particularly introverted Obligers—prefer impersonal forms of accountability, such as an app or a paid coach who communicates by email.

Also, for some Obligers, accountability works better when it's positive. Reminders and oversight feel like nagging, and nagging may trigger Obliger-rebellion. These Obligers do much better when accountability takes the form of praise, cheers, and encouragement. One Obliger explained, "When I tell someone to hold me accountable, it's like my fate rests in their hands. But when I ask for some high-energy high fives, I feel supported and therefore powerful. Cheering also feels less invasive."

So here's the vital question: How do Obligers create accountability?

Accountability Partner

Obligers can team up with an accountability partner: a classmate, trainer, personal organizer, coach, health-care worker, teacher, family member, or friend. In one study, people who enrolled in a weight-loss program with an accountability partner maintained their weight loss more successfully than people who joined alone.

Some Obligers report using their children as their accountability partners. One study found that when a group of children was trained as "change agents," their mothers lost significantly more weight and got more physical activity than the mothers in a control group.

Unfortunately, however, informal accountability partners can be unreliable. If that partner loses interest, gets distracted, or doesn't want to play the enforcer, the Obliger stalls out. An Obliger lamented, "It really frustrates me when my writing buddy admits that she hasn't been working on her novel, because then I feel like I don't need to write, either."

Sometimes, too, Obligers try to recruit people to act as accountability partners—but those people don't always cooperate. For instance, Upholders are often reluctant to provide others with accountability. As an Upholder explained:

I get frustrated with my Obliger husband. He talks about going back to school, finding a new job, etc., but won't do anything. And I won't nag him about it, because, darn it, if he wants it, he should just do it. Why wouldn't he? Even though it would be more likely to happen, and he probably wouldn't even mind, if I did some selective nagging on the topic.

Her Obliger husband would probably welcome the external accountability, but she doesn't want to have to provide it.

Because it can be tough to find a reliable accountability partner among friends and family, Obligers may do better with a professional. For instance, coaches—career coaches, health coaches, life coaches—can provide the crucial accountability by setting concrete goals, establishing deadlines, and looking over their clients' shoulders. They're paid to do this, so they don't flake out. This costs money, of course, but it may also be the key to unleashing an Obliger's potential.

Accountability Groups

People who don't want to pay for a professional or rely on a single accountability partner can join or start an accountability group. An accountability group might be made up of friends, family members, coworkers, or strangers brought together by a common desire to hold one another accountable. As Alcoholics Anonymous, Weight Watchers, law school study groups, and Happiness Project groups demonstrate, we give and get accountability, as well as energy and ideas, from meeting with like-directed people.

For many Obligers, face-to-face interactions work best, but when that's not practical, technology can be an important tool. A myriad of platforms, apps, and groups exist to help people hold one another accountable—including my own Better app, which is designed to make it easy to form accountability groups of all kinds. Virtual accountability is less intense but more convenient.

Obligers need to take care when forming an accountability group. As one Obliger told me, "Before realizing I was an Obliger, I often ended up doing more than my share of the work running groups and holding groups together. I got burned out, went into Obliger-Rebellion mode. People from other Tendencies have different reasons for joining groups, and Obligers need to be careful about who we form groups with."

A Client, Customer, or Employee

Clients and customers impose accountability by the very nature of the relationship. An Obliger told me, "I'd been putting off creating an online training course to accompany my podcast on self-publishing. In my latest episode, I offered a free copy of the training course, when it's ready, to the first 25 listeners who sign up. Because people have signed up, I actually have to create the course."

Similarly, an Obliger explained, "I didn't invite people over because my apartment wasn't clean. So I decided to invite friends over, and I was able to clean it. I was aware of this pattern before I read your book, but I thought of it as 'shame motivation.' I like your term of 'external accountability' much better."

A friend told me that her Obliger mother got herself to exercise by becoming a fitness instructor; I've spoken to many such Obligers who sought a paid or volunteer job as an accountability strategy.

On the flip side, an Obliger can hire an employee to create

accountability. "I use a 'hire a teenager' strategy for cleaning out the storage area, dealing with overdue yard work, and so on," an Obliger told me. "Hiring someone makes me set a date and time, I'm less likely to cancel with someone I've hired than I would be with my family, and paying someone makes me get serious."

Benefit to Others

Obligers can often do things for others that they can't do for themselves, so an Obliger may be able to meet an aim by thinking of its benefit to other people instead of its personal value. For instance, many Obligers have told me that they were able to leave a bad marriage only after they realized that they had to protect their kids.

An Obliger wrote, "I'm the controller of a company, and to create accountability, I tie my personal commitments to my commitment to work: if I get enough sleep, I work better; if I exercise, I have more energy and spend less time at the chiropractor."

Another Obliger told me, "Even though it should grate against my feminist sensibilities, I pack my boyfriend (and myself incidentally) a lunch every day because I'd never maintain the habit if he weren't counting on me."

Obligers can meet an expectation if it's tied to their duty to be a good role model. An Obliger had a creative solution: "I've made a family rule that when I'm at home, whenever I look at my phone, my kids can look at their phones."

Obligers have come up with ingenious ways to benefit others—for their own benefit. One Obliger told me, "My wife loves to exercise. I don't like it. So we agreed that she can't exercise unless I've exercised the day before. I'd feel guilty if I deprived her of it." Another explained: "My sister-in-law and I made a list of healthy habits we want to cultivate. If we both stick with the plan, we'll earn a spa day. The catch is that since we're Obligers, we earn the spa day for each other. If I don't follow through, she won't get her spa day—and vice versa. We'd let ourselves down, but we'd never let each other down."

Sometimes Obligers use the future to create their sense of accountability. For a long time, I was puzzled when people told me things like "I'm keeping this journal for my kids, after I'm gone" or "I'm maintaining this garden as a legacy for my kids"—because I figured that those kids won't want to read fifteen years' worth of their father's journals, and they'll never live in that house with the big garden. But now I realize that this doing-it-for-my-kids strategy can help Obligers accomplish something worthwhile.

Many Obligers struggle to say no even when they're feeling very burdened by expectations. To overcome this reluctance, Obligers can remind themselves that saying no to one person allows them to say yes to someone else. "My team always wanted to work late," a friend told me, "and I didn't want to let them down. But we had a family discussion about how we want to eat dinner together. Now I can say no to the team, because otherwise I'll be disappointing my wife and kids."

Another Obliger, a highly regarded professor, accepted too many speaking engagements, until one day he thought, "If I turn down the keynote talk, I'll give someone else the chance to speak." That thought allowed him to decline some speaking requests.

As an Upholder, when I hear someone say, "I realized I need to do this so I can be a better parent/employee/friend," I think, "No, do it for yourself!" But for Obligers, doing something for other people helps them do it for themselves.

Oher Creative Accountability Devices

I've been astonished by the creativity shown by Obligers seeking accountability. After a book talk, a young man told me, "I exercise with a buddy, and after every workout, we each leave with one of the other person's sneakers. That way, if I don't show up, he can't work out." My very favorite accountability device came from the Obliger who told me, "I wanted to get up earlier, but I live alone. So I created an embarrassing Facebook post and use Hootsuite to set it to post every morning at 8:00 a.m. unless I get up ahead of time to disable it."

No matter what kind of a task that an Obliger wants to meet, and no matter what individual temperament an Obliger may have, there's some way to create outer accountability. As one music teacher wrote me, "I have many suggestions to help my Obliger music students practice consistently: join a band or an orchestra (especially effective if the student has a special role, such as the bass clarinet in a quartet); become a mentor for a younger musician; organize practice sessions in pairs, where a failure to show up will hurt a fellow student; or make a pact with a loved one that that person can't do some desirable activity unless the Obliger has practiced."

It's worth repeating, yet again: To meet inner expectations, Obligers must find some source of outer accountability.

Consider the example of William Shawn, *The New Yorker*'s legendary editor. In Lillian Ross's memoir *Here But Not Here,* Shawn clearly emerges as an Obliger.

Shawn was a powerful, well-regarded editor who lived

with his wife and three children, and for forty years, with his wife's knowledge, he also had a home with Ross.

Shawn would appear to be someone who had exactly the life he wanted. However, Ross writes that Shawn felt trapped in his role as editor—he wanted to do his own writing—but felt he had to stay in his job because: "There was no one else who could have kept the magazine alive . . . I could not abandon all those people." Occasionally he told Ross, "It's someone else's life that I have lived." Although Shawn and Ross had a passionate relationship, he split his life between the two households. Ross writes, "I agreed that he could not leave Cecille . . . Cecille wanted him to be sitting there no matter what."

So how might Obliger Shawn have built the life he wanted? If he'd signed a book deal with an editor, he would've had deadlines and accountability, and he might have done his own writing. If he'd told himself, "I should give my editors the opportunity to prove themselves," he might have delegated some magazine responsibilities. If he'd said to Ross, "You need to help me end my marriage," they could have done it—together.

When Outer Accountability Disappears

On the subject of outer accountability, I've often read the argument that authoritarian institutions, such as the military, dismantle people's inner architecture of self-command. For instance, in his autobiography *World Within World,* poet Stephen Spender observed, "As with most soldiers, the army had disciplined him at the price of breaking down any power of self-discipline which he might once have possessed. Outside the Army he seemed lacking in will and purpose, because these had been forced upon him by punishments and drills."

But I think Spender misunderstands the dynamic. I suspect that when an institution supplies a lot of external accountability, it doesn't break down Obligers' self-discipline; it simply makes it unnecessary for Obligers to develop their own personal systems of external accountability. In ordinary life, many Obligers realize they need accountability in order to succeed. But when an institution supplies outer accountability, the Obligers don't need to do it for themselves—and when they're released from that institution's expectations, they often struggle.

Being set free from well-established outer expectations— established by a corporate job, training program, religious order, or school—can be risky for Obligers. They might be perfectly productive, with healthy habits, when they're in an environment that supplies external accountability, but then become paralyzed—without really understanding why— when those expectations disappear. An Obliger wrote, "In my former job, I led a big team. I was known as the guy who could get anything done. But once I struck out on my own, with no employees to be responsible for, I started having problems with follow-through."

Along the same lines, a friend who works in education told me, "Some charter schools tell the kids exactly what to do—what to wear, how to work, how to spend their time. And some kids do great in that environment but fall apart when they go to college."

"There are probably lots of factors," I said, "but I wonder if one problem is that Obliger kids get the accountability they need until they get to college, where it can feel like no one cares what you're doing."

Or an Obliger might do fine in college but drift after graduation. Plans like "In the fall, I'll apply to med school," "I'll send out résumés," "I'll write a novel," or "I'll apply for a grant" may come to nothing with no classes to attend, papers to complete, grades to earn, or professors to please.

Similarly, an Obliger who quits a full-time job to work on an entrepreneurial venture may stall out, or an Obliger between jobs can get stuck, or an Obliger who becomes an empty-nester may feel lost.

The solution? External accountability.

How Obligers Can Manage the Pros and Cons of the Tendency

Some Obligers embrace the Obliger Tendency; they see it as a virtue and a strength.

For instance, many Obligers characterize their behavior as "client first"—a reason for pride. An Obliger told me decisively: "I'm there for my clients, no matter what. That gives me my edge. That's the way I am, that's the way I want to be, and that's the attitude I want from the people who work for me." Another agreed, "I'm a great 'gun for hire.' I consider my responsibilities toward the company, my colleagues, and our clients as pretty holy and definitely above and beyond my own needs."

This attitude may prevail at work and also at home. Many Obligers have told me, again with great satisfaction, "The needs of my family come first, always."

Certainly many religious teachings emphasize the Obliger way.

But while some Obligers appreciate their Tendency, it's

also true that Obligers are more likely than Upholders, Questioners, or Rebels to say that they wish they belonged to a different Tendency. Why?

With the other three Tendencies, much of the frustration they create falls on others, not themselves. People may get annoyed by stickler Upholders, or interrogator Questioners, or maverick Rebels—but that's their problem. With Obligers, it's the Obligers themselves who bear the brunt of the downsides of their Tendency. They're often vexed by the fact that they can meet others' expectations but not their expectations for themselves.

One Obliger wrote, "I have no trouble getting my work done for my job, and I'm a great friend who's always willing to help, but at the end of the day, I often ask: 'What did you do today to help make your dreams come true?' And, unfortunately, the answer is often a big fat 'Nothing.'"

Sometimes, when I point out to Obligers that external accountability is the key to meeting inner expectations, they aren't relieved to discover a straightforward solution; instead, they resent being dependent on a system of outer accountability.

When I was giving a talk about the Four Tendencies, an Obliger asked, "Can't an Obliger become an Upholder? I want to hold myself to my own expectations, I don't want to depend on outer accountability. That feels weak."

"Well," I said gingerly, "it seems to me that it's very hard to change a fundamental aspect of your nature—if it's even possible at all. But it's very easy to figure out ways to give yourself external accountability. So why not take the easy way?"

Rather than focus on the downside of the Obliger Tendency, Obligers can find ways to counterbalance it through accountability.

Different Obligers interpret their same actions in different ways; it all depends on their perspective. One Obliger says, "Well, I'm twenty pounds overweight, and I never exercise, and I really should go to the dentist, but I never let anything slide in the office, and I'm a great husband and a great father who's always there for my family. I feel good about myself." Another says, "Well, I never let anything slide in the office, and I'm a great wife and a great mother who's always there for my family, but I'm twenty pounds overweight, and I never exercise, and I really should go to the dentist. I feel bad about myself."

But whether they embrace or regret their Obliger Tendency, Obligers often misinterpret their patterns of behavior. Even when they grasp that they're meeting outer expectations and failing to meet inner expectations, they misdiagnose the reason.

Some Obligers chalk it up to dedication and intensity. "I can't do something for myself if there's something I could be doing for my clients—and there's always something I can be doing for my clients."

Some Obligers take great macho pride in the lengths to which they'll go to meet expectations. A reader told me about her Obliger boss, "Her doctor told her to stay in the hospital, but she left after spine surgery to attend a work dinner. She's always doing things like that."

Other Obligers attribute their behavior to self-sacrifice. "I always meet other people's priorities at the expense of my own priorities," "I can't take time for myself," "People tell me I should be more selfish."

Or Obligers may assume their behavior is due to low self-esteem, or lack of motivation, or because of some character flaw.

A friend who was procrastinating about taking course work needed to advance his career said, "I'm lazy, that's my problem."

"That's not true!" I protested. "You meet every work deadline. You're in a running club. Right?"

"Well, right," he admitted reluctantly.

"Your problem can't be laziness. It's something else."

The Obliger pattern is not an issue of self-sacrifice, self-esteem, boundaries, motivation, people-pleasing, or discipline, but rather—and I repeat it yet again—an issue of external accountability.

Because Obligers often misunderstand the patterns of Obliger behavior, they're prone to a common, sometimes serious mistake. Obligers expect that if they could only free themselves from some burdensome outer expectation—for instance, by leaving a demanding job—they'd then find it easy to meet their expectations for themselves.

Warning! In most cases, without the addition of some sort of external accountability, the absence of external expectations doesn't help Obligers meet their inner expectations. As one Obliger told me, "Trying to clear space in your life for your own goals doesn't work for an Obliger. I made that mistake for years."

It's crucial that Obligers recognize this need for outer accountability; otherwise they may make major life changes in the hope of meeting inner expectations—which then doesn't happen. For instance, a reader wrote on my blog:

> I have a Ph.D. (thanks to my many Obliger qualities), but I was so burned out by five years of writing about stuff that mattered lots to others and nothing to me, that I decided to take some time for myself and for my goals. Mainly, I

wanted to lose weight, write my second book, start a blog, do a relief project, and complete the renovations on my house. So far, the book has not been started, neither has the blog, I've gained fourteen pounds, and I've given up on doing the relief project anytime soon. However, the house project is actually moving along quite nicely, because I know how happy it makes my husband to see it progress.

Another Obliger posted his strikingly similar postretirement experience:

After a twenty-five-year career of successful public service, plus raising two daughters with my wife, I was really looking forward to retirement. Finally, an opportunity to pursue my own interests and activities. I even sacrificed some retirement income in exchange for retiring five years early.

Almost immediately, I found I couldn't find the motivation to pursue the activities I knew I would enjoy: attend classes, get to the gym, complete some home improvements.

I did manage one thing: I joined a hiking club and hike most Wednesday and Saturday mornings. I now see that it's the external expectation: knowing that people are waiting for me to meet them enables me to get my gear ready the night before and be out the door at 7 a.m.

But as I repeatedly failed to implement any other personal goal, I was becoming increasingly disappointed in myself. What a relief to learn the Four Tendencies. I may be able to figure out a way to do these things after all.

An Obliger told me, "We Obligers take care of others before ourselves." And it was all I could do to stop myself from shouting, "No, no!" I managed to stay calm and say, "I don't think it's the case that Obligers take care of others first, and then just run out of time and energy before they turn to themselves. Fact is, they meet outer expectations but not inner expectations. It's a very big difference."

Once Obligers grasp the true pattern of their Tendency, they can figure out ways to harness its strengths and offset its weaknesses. One Obliger told me, "Now that I know I'm an Obliger, instead of going against my grain, I'm letting the grain be my guide."

How Obligers Shift the Line Between Outer and Inner Expectations

Obligers respond to outer expectations and struggle to meet inner expectations, but different Obligers draw the line between outer and inner in different ways, and that line can also shift depending on circumstances—say, with family.

For instance, for many Obligers, spouses or family count as part of themselves, so their spouses' expectations become "inner" expectations and are therefore ignored. A Questioner wrote in frustration: "My husband is willing to treat me just as poorly as he treats himself. I'm not kidding. I want him to be better to himself *and* to me."

My sister, Elizabeth, told me, "I've learned that if we need to do something like send someone a check, I'm better off forwarding the email with the request to Adam rather than emailing him myself. He's more likely to do it if the request comes from the outside."

Sometimes context decides whether a family member seems to be "inner" or "outer." An Obliger friend is an attentive father who usually views his responsibility to his children as an outer expectation and readily lives up to it. However, he's in the client-service business, and when business obligations conflict with family obligations, the client prevails, as the more "outer."

The shifting nature of inner vs. outer can cause trouble in a marriage. One reader wrote:

> I'm an Obliger, and the conflicts in our marriage happen when we're around other people. Then I change from obliging my husband's wishes to obliging the other people we're with. This confuses my husband; he's used to me obliging his whims. Also, I treat my husband as I treat myself, which means his needs/demands take a backseat to whatever the other couple needs/wants. Ah, the fights we've had without ever getting at the nut of the problem.

Also, if an Obliger considers family expectations to be "inner" expectations, a family member won't make an effective source of outer accountability.

One Obliger, a highly successful businessman, told me, "For years, my wife kept saying, 'Take time for yourself, go to the gym, you do everything for the company, you owe it to yourself to go to the doctor, yada, yada, yada.' I never listened. Who has time for that? Then the chairman of my board said, 'Ed, we've got a lot of big things coming up this year, and you look like you're going to have a heart attack any minute. Too much depends on you. Lose weight, get some exercise, get some rest, go to the doctor.' So I did."

How to Understand and Protect Against
Obliger-Rebellion

Obligers often feel exploited—*and they are*. Because, after all, when it comes time to ask for someone's help, whom do we ask? An Upholder, a Questioner, a Rebel—or an Obliger? Obligers, of course, because they're the most likely to lend a hand. In her essay "The Rage Cage," writer Caroline Knapp tells a very Obliger-y story:

> A friend asked me to walk her dog, a favor that sounds benign enough but actually infuriated me. Her reasons for asking annoyed me: her partner had the flu, which meant that she'd had to walk the dog twice the day before; she was also busy writing a paper for school, so taking the dog out twice for a second day felt unduly burdensome. I stood there while she told me this, and I thought: Wait a minute; I walk my dog twice a day every day, and I'm always on deadline; and this request feels both ludicrous and insulting to me. But instead of telling her to suck it up and walk her own dog, I sucked it up: picked the animal up at 6:30 a.m., dutifully trotted her around Fresh Pond, delivered her back to her owners, and walked around for the rest of the week feeling put-upon, taken advantage of, and—well, angry.

If that neighbor had asked an Upholder, a Questioner, or a Rebel who didn't want to walk the dog, the answer would have been no. As an Upholder, I would've thought, "Sorry, I've got my own responsibilities to meet." A Questioner would've asked the question, "Why should I walk your dog, when I'm even busier than you are?" A Rebel would've thought, "I don't want to do that, so I won't." Here's the thing: The neighbor knew to ask an Obliger because Obligers are the good neighbors who help you out of a jam by walking your dog, even when they have their own dogs and their own work and their own deadlines.

Not only do the other Tendencies ignore expectations that an Obliger feels obliged to meet, they're often *unsympathetic* to the Obligers. While Obligers may view their action as admirable—"I put other people's needs before my own"— the other Tendencies may not see it this way. Upholders, Questioners, and Rebels say things like "If playing the guitar every day is important to you, stop talking about it and just do it." "Well, if you don't want to do the assignment, why did you agree to do it?" "You say that we have to attend every client dinner, but I disagree, so I won't go."

Because of such attitudes, Obligers often feel both resentful and unappreciated. An Obliger might consider an Upholder, Questioner, or Rebel to be self-centered and selfish—and Upholders and Questioners *are* self-centered and self-ish, in the sense that the aims of the "self," which are inner expectations, are at the core of what they do. Rebels also seem self-centered, but for different reasons.

Another reason that Obligers are susceptible to feeling burned out and exploited? They often have trouble delegating certain tasks. For some reason, a particular assignment must be done by that Obliger himself or herself; it can't be outsourced. They think, "No one else will do this, so now it's been left to me" or "No one can do this as well as I can."

After I mentioned this aspect of Obligerness at a talk, a guy came up to me afterward. "My wife is an Obliger, and you described this thing that drives me crazy," he said. "She insists that we invite her extended family over for Thanksgiving, and then she complains about all the work—the cooking, the cleanup. I say, 'Let's hire a caterer and cleaning help,' but she refuses. But then she wants *me* to help! I don't want to cook or clean. I tell her, 'If you don't want to do the work, don't invite so many people. Or pay someone else to do the work. But if you invite them and choose to do it yourself, stop complaining! And don't drag *me* into it.'"

I offered a suggestion. "You could say, 'If you're busy doing all this work, you don't have time to catch up with your family and make them feel welcome. We only see them a few times a year. Let's hire some people to help out, so you can give your attention to your relatives.' Or you could say, 'You wear yourself out cooking, and then you're distracted and tired and understandably, you get crabby. Let's make holiday time nicer for everyone, and hire a caterer. I'll be disappointed if you don't follow up on my suggestion.'"

An Obliger friend told me about his wife's way of getting around his Obligerness. "My wife understands me perfectly. I felt like I should mow our lawn myself, though I hated doing it, often have to work on the weekends, and was always putting off the job, which made her mad. But I also refused to call a lawn service. Then one day my wife came home and said, 'I told the neighbor's son that he could mow the lawn. He needs money for college.' Now I don't want to disappoint the kid."

This Obliger issue comes up often in an office environment. Obligers often find it hard to say no and may have trouble delegating—which can lead to bottlenecks and burnout. Obligers should watch out for this pattern and find ways to delegate or manage those responsibilities.

Because they're susceptible to feeling neglected or exploited, Obligers sometimes show a striking, harmful pattern. If they feel overwhelmed by relentless external pressure,

Obligers may reach a point of Obliger-rebellion, where they simply refuse to meet some expectation—often dramatically and without warning. In Obliger-rebellion, an Obliger who has been meeting expectations suddenly decides, "No more!" and refuses.

Obliger-rebellion may be a one-time action or it can become a consistent pattern of behavior; it can take the form of minor, almost hidden refusals—or dramatic, life-changing explosions.

Tennis superstar Andre Agassi's outstanding memoir, *Open*, reveals him to be a textbook Obliger who displays Obliger-rebellion. He's able to meet others' expectations (his father's demand that he excels at tennis; his girlfriend Brooke Shields's desire to get married) but struggles to meet his expectations for himself. He shows his Obliger-rebellion in small, symbolic ways, such as defying tennis tradition by wearing denim shorts and sporting a mullet, actions that he describes as "thrashing against the lack of choice in my life." Agassi demonstrates the tremendous energy and accomplishment that Obligers can bring to bear, and also the resentment that can arise from Obligers' feeling that they're working toward others' expectations.

Speaking of famous Obliger athletes, Tiger Woods is also an Obliger who experienced spectacular Obliger-rebellion. He repeatedly told members of his circle that he wanted to leave golf to become a Navy SEAL; they prevailed on him to fulfill their expectations of him as a golf star; he rebelled.

Many circumstances can eventually trigger Obliger-rebellion. Expectations that:

- are unrealistically ambitious—"You can break the sales record this year!"

131

- are unfair, because others aren't doing their share—"While you're at it, could you proofread my report, too?"

- are accompanied by shaming—"It's pathetic to see how messy you keep your room."

- are nagging or disapproving—"Are you finally going to the gym today?"

- involve tasks that are distasteful or ungratifying—"You need to start making cold calls."

- deprive the Obliger of getting credit for a personal success—"You're losing weight on this program because I'm telling you what to do."

- are imposed by people who are hard to please or who don't matter to the Obliger—"If this is the best work you can manage to do, I guess we'll have to send it to the client."

- trigger feelings of being taken for granted or exploited—"You'll stay late again tonight, won't you?"

- are demands that don't reflect an Obliger's true aims for himself or herself—"With your aptitude for science, you'd be a great doctor. You have to go to medical school."

- become the final straw—"We're downsizing, so now you need to handle ten additional clients."

- unleash feelings of guilt or embarrassment—"You must announce your blood sugar levels to the entire group."

Obligers are often puzzled by their episodes of Obliger-rebellion. They don't understand their behavior, they can't control it, they feel like they're acting out of character. One

Obliger described Obliger-rebellion as "The Big 'No' That Kinda Wrecks My Life for a While."

Another Obliger said:

> I'm an ambitious Ph.D. candidate about a year from finishing my doctorate in molecular biology, and for the first time in my life, I've turned in projects that were completed halfheartedly or late. I feel like an alien has invaded my body. I've begun to ask: Why am I acting this way? What's changed? Or the scariest and most honest yet, why am I getting my doctorate? Realizing that I'm an Obliger has helped me see that I've been working for my Ph.D. mostly to fulfill the external expectations of my wife, family, friends, and academic advisers—not my own true goals.

As this comment illustrates, Obliger-rebellion can erupt not just when Obligers feel exploited but also when they realize that they're meeting expectations established by others, which aren't truly fulfilling.

One contributor to Obliger-rebellion? Too often, Obligers don't protest against a troublesome situation—such as unfair division of labor, exploitation, or lack of credit. And why not? Because they think they shouldn't have to protest; they imagine that others must realize the oppressiveness of the burdens being imposed—and will, or should, lift those burdens without any word from them. That is, *the Obliger expects others to know to stop imposing their expectations, without prompting, to provide relief for the Obliger.* But very often that doesn't happen, and then the Obliger becomes furious that others have imposed those heavy expectations even when the Obliger hasn't objected to those expectations.

And why don't other people ease up? As noted, the other

Tendencies don't experience the same heavy weight of outer expectations that Obligers do, so they're not aware of the painful burden they're imposing; also, the other Tendencies have their own ways of resisting outer expectations, so they expect Obligers to resist as well: "If you didn't want to do it, why did you agree to do it?" "If you can't meet your own deadline, why did you agree to take on that extra work?"

In Obliger-rebellion, instead of giving others the opportunity to fix a situation, Obligers persist without protest, until they suddenly rebel. Obliger-rebellion can cause people to walk out on jobs—and also on marriages and friendships—without warning. One Obliger recalled:

> My rebellions have been quiet, deadly, and permanent. Two friendships, one job, and one marriage have gone the way of Obliger-rebellion. I experience it as a flip of a switch. After months of meeting what I thought were unreasonable and unappreciated expectations in a job, one Monday I called an alternative employer, and that afternoon I resigned. I didn't want to have a discussion, even when I was asked, "What can we do to get you to stay?"
>
> "You're dead to me now"—that's exactly what it's like, even with a marriage of eighteen years. After many years of propping up that relationship, I woke one morning knowing, with absolute clarity, that I was done, and there's no way back.
>
> While I don't regret any of these rebellions, I'm grateful to have a conceptual framework, because I can see the benefits of recognizing warning signs. And I can acknowledge that my willingness to oblige, to take up the slack, comes with this risk.

Of course, a person of any Tendency might decide to end a relationship. But with Obliger-rebellion, it's abrupt—the

Obliger keeps meeting expectations that seem unreasonable until the "snap." One Obliger described Obliger-rebellion: "I'm a bomb exploding, and I have no control of the devastation." Other Obligers use words like "simmer," "fester," "eat away," "boil over," "erupt," and "volcano" to describe the feelings accompanying Obliger-rebellion.

While Obliger-rebellion can be very dramatic, it can also take the form of symbolic acts or small gestures. One Obliger wrote, "A coworker always comments if I'm a few minutes late. It makes me so mad that I'll sometimes sit in my car for a minute instead of rushing in. I feel terrible about being late, but it just ticks me off that he says that to me so often. The more he says it, the less I'm on time."

Odd side note: Being deliberately late is a popular form of Obliger-rebellion. In fact, on the Better app, someone sent me the link to this Superluxe T-shirt, very appropriate for Obligers in Obliger-rebellion:

While some Obligers manage to channel their Obliger-rebellion into acts that, although rebellious, won't cause much damage, some Obliger-rebellion causes self-sabotage. One Obliger explained, "I do something that will hurt me instead of those who are asking, demanding, or even just advising, me to do something. For example, I've gone into presentations or interviews unprepared. It's like I'm obliging while rebelling—I don't hurt anyone but myself."

Sometimes Obliger-rebellion encompasses an entire field of expectations—often in the context of *health*. One Obliger wrote:

> When it comes to work, church and other volunteer organizations, social interactions, childrearing, I tend to do what's expected of me. But the faintest whiff of expectation, obligation, or constraint when it comes to weight loss or exercise sends me screaming in the other direction. I can't tell you how much money I've squandered on gym and weight-loss club memberships—and ended up never going to the gym or quitting the program, most often gaining weight in the process.

Perhaps health is such a frequent target of Obliger-rebellion because it's an area where other people press and nag and admonish, so that expectations feel externally imposed, yet the health consequences fall wholly on the Obligers.

As I studied the results of the representative sample, I was intrigued to see that Obligers were just as likely as Rebels to agree with the statement "My doctor has told me why it's important that I make a certain change in my life, but I haven't done it." It's easy to see why Rebels might reject "doctor's orders," but it's more surprising to see that answer from Obligers. I think it's due to two factors: one, Obligers don't always have the accountability needed to accomplish that change; two, Obligers may be showing Obliger-rebellion against a health expectation.

But while Obliger-rebellion sometimes makes it harder for Obligers to be healthy, happy, and successful, Obliger-rebellion is also an important form of *self-protection*. Obliger-rebellion can act as a vital emergency escape hatch; it allows the Obliger to break free from that hated job, unbearable spouse, difficult relationship, or burdensome obligation. Obliger-rebellion is the safety valve that relieves the excessive pressure that's crushing the Obliger.

Usually, after some time passes, the spell of Obliger-rebellion lifts, even if nothing much has changed. Better, however, to safeguard against Obliger-rebellion, by helping Obligers avoid burnout and resentment in the first place.

So what can be done about Obliger-rebellion?

Once Obligers recognize this behavior pattern, they can take steps to relieve the pressure by watching for signs that resentment is building and then *saying something about it:* "Can we take a look to see how the extra shifts are being distributed?" "I'm already on three committees," "One person can't manage both kids' schedules this weekend, so we need to divvy things up."

Because Obligers are so susceptible to burnout, the people around Obligers—family, friends, colleagues, health-care professionals, and so on—all have a role to play in helping them to avoid that state. We can set up systems that encourage them to say no, delegate, take breaks, turn down requests, make time for themselves, and so on. One Questioner wrote:

> My fiancé is an Obliger, and often it feels like we do a lot of the things I'd like to do and not much that he'd like to do. Lately, to make things more fair, on Saturday mornings we each sit down and list the three to five things we'd like to accomplish during the weekend. Then we make it our goal to

get all of it accomplished. He now expresses what he wants to do, and we've created accountability for him, because I ask about his list.

Once Obligers slide into Obliger-rebellion, they need relief from expectations, but paradoxically, they may need external expectations to get that relief. A manager who sees that an Obliger is overburdened might remove a responsibility from that Obliger's portfolio or reprimand coworkers for dumping too much work on the Obliger.

Because it can be so dramatic, Obliger-rebellion shows up frequently in fiction and movies—the most famous example is probably the classic Christmas movie *It's a Wonderful Life*. George Bailey (James Stewart) is an Obliger who, at every juncture, meets outer expectations but not inner expectations. Significantly, when George finally drops into Obliger-rebellion, it's aimed at himself—in this case, he almost throws himself off a bridge. But, sadly, most Obligers don't have an angel like Clarence to help them. George Bailey also illustrates a common Obliger pattern of believing that he must personally meet a certain expectation. Why shouldn't George's younger brother, Harry, take his turn running the Bailey Building & Loan, as agreed—or if Harry didn't want to do it, why wasn't that Harry's problem to solve?

SUMMARY: OBLIGER

LIKELY STRENGTHS:

Good boss, responsive leader, team player

Feels great obligation to meet others' expectations

Responsible

Willing to go the extra mile

Responds to outer accountability

POSSIBLE WEAKNESSES:

Susceptible to overwork and burnout

May show the destructive pattern of Obliger-rebellion

Exploitable

May become resentful

Has trouble saying no or imposing limits

8

Dealing with
an Obliger

"Say yes to less"

Work • Spouse • Child • Health Client • Choosing a
Career

Dealing with an Obliger at Work

In many cases, Obligers make excellent colleagues and bosses.
They follow through, they pitch in when other people need
help, they volunteer for optional assignments, they're flexible
when things need to change.

Obligers respond to the expectations that work situations
almost inevitably supply—with deadlines, evaluations, and
deliverables. In the rarer case where accountability doesn't
appear naturally, it's crucial to supply it. Vague exhortations
to get something done often have no effect.

A writer friend, an Obliger, recalled: "When I signed the
contract to write a memoir, I told my editor, 'I can only write
when I have to turn in something. Please give me some fake
deadlines along the way.' But he said, 'Don't worry, the book
will be great, you'll get it done, blah, blah.' He just kept being
so understanding."

GRETCHEN RUBIN

"What happened?" I asked.

"I wrote the whole thing the three weeks before it was due. It could've been so much better if I'd started earlier."

Out of misguided consideration, the editor had refused to provide accountability. If he'd understood that this writer was an Obliger, he could've taken a different approach.

When people request accountability in any context, they should get it; people ask for it because they know they need it. One Obliger told me, "I told my supervisor that I need a tough, demanding boss. I get more done, I do better work."

Because Obligers put such a high value on meeting outer expectations, others may take advantage of them, and if they feel exploited and overworked, Obligers may fall into Obliger-rebellion, which is tough for managers and supervisors to handle. One Obliger said:

> I'm a nurse, and my unit has constant staffing issues with sick calls, busy shifts, etc. I've been there three years, and my boss senses those of us who are Obligers and abuses us by constantly asking us to pick up extra shifts. It's very frustrating, because several nurses who are always "out sick" are posting on Facebook all day long while we're working. For a long time, I did help the unit, but it led to personal burnout, and now I'm in a full-scale rebellion and always say no.

As this example illustrates, Obligers often struggle to say no, until they say a big NO, which can be a real problem.

Because Obligers are often very valuable employees, it's crucial that managers watch out for Obligers, to make sure to ward off Obliger-rebellion, so that a valuable employee doesn't get fed up and quit without notice.

To avoid an Obliger-rebellion, a boss, employee, or co-worker can help Obligers establish limits and boundaries:

—**Remind the Obliger that saying no allows him or her to say yes to work that's more important:** "I need your report on Friday, and if you keep getting dragged into other people's meetings, you'll miss the deadline."

—**Enforce limits to prevent burnout and Obliger-rebellion:** "You're entitled to a vacation, and I'm going to make sure you take it."

—**Stop others from exploiting the Obliger:** "We're all up against the deadline, so everyone on this team needs to do his or her own final edits."

—**Point to the Obliger's duty as a role model:** "If you stay until 9:00 p.m., you set a bad example for your staff."

—**Take work away from the Obliger, if the Obliger has taken on too much:** A friend who heads a finance firm told me, "I have a very valuable employee—he's the best. Everyone wants to work with him, because he makes people look good, but he can't keep saying yes to everyone. It's not sustainable. At his last review, I said, 'You're doing too much work, too well, and I mean that as a sincere criticism.' He couldn't delegate, he couldn't step back. So we took him off a big account, and he's doing much better."

Obligers often make terrific bosses and great, even visionary leaders, because they feel such obligation to their organization; they're responsive and responsible. As with people in all the Tendencies, however, they may struggle to understand the thinking of those who don't share their Tendency. One Obliger wrote: "I'm an Obliger, and as a manager, I find it hard when people say no to me or question everything." It's challenging to manage people who are different from ourselves—and the first step is to acknowledge that difference.

The instinct to meet outer expectations may get Obliger bosses into trouble. One Upholder friend told me of his frustration at a new job. "My boss is clearly an extreme Obliger," he told me. "She's the CEO, but she drops everything to help a client or an employee, and it's draining our productivity. Nothing gets done."

Obligers face particular challenges when they want to work solo. They may be superbly productive at the office, but when they try to go out on their own, they may stall out, because of the lack of outer accountability. So, if Obligers want to start their own business, they must establish, from the very beginning, a system of accountability. Accountability can come from a business coach, from a mentor, from customers, clients, or students (even if they aren't paying—yet), or from a group on the Better app—it doesn't matter, but that accountability must come from *somewhere*.

Once established as entrepreneurs, Obligers may find it easy to meet the external commitments of their work— meeting client deadlines, filing taxes, answering the phone— yet struggle with inner-generated tasks, such as networking, building the business, or saying no to requests that waste their time or to clients who are overly demanding. As always, the solution is to find external systems of deadlines and boundaries.

Dealing with an Obliger Spouse

Obligers make great spouses because they put so much value in meeting others' expectations. It's important that their spouses recognize Obliger patterns, however.

For instance, if an Obliger asks a spouse to act as an accountability partner, the spouse should provide that accountability or figure out another way to supply it. One Obliger explained, "I work out every day by getting my husband to ask me about it when he gets home. He's superencouraging if I don't, so I feel more driven to do it the next day. Health is important to him, so this makes me follow through. It's crazy, because even though I've set this up, I feel the urge to conquer the task, just because he asks."

Husbands and wives also have a role to play in helping their spouses to ward off Obliger burnout and Obliger-rebellion by providing the external accountability needed to limit the Obligers' sense of obligation. "You need a nap. For my sake, please go lie down."

One Obliger said, "My husband offers to watch the kids so that I can go to a Spin class that I love on Saturday mornings, but somehow I just can't get myself to go." Her husband could help by saying, "Don't you want to set a good example for the kids by sticking to your healthy commitment?" Or: "It's nice for me and the kids to have this special time together each week." Appeals to Obliger values help Obligers follow through.

One podcast listener wrote:

Knowing my husband is an Obliger has been a real revelation. It's great because he's so kind, but I've realized I need to

145

"protect" his personal commitments. If I ask, he would easily drop a personal commitment to help me. I need to look
out for him so he doesn't drop anything too important. His
former wife took advantage of his obliging nature, so I tend
to set boundaries for him.

By "setting boundaries" for her husband—helping him
to say no (even to her) and preventing others from exploiting him—this wife helps to thwart possible Obliger-rebellion
in her husband. The people around Obligers can help ward
off Obliger-rebellion by anticipating it. If one spouse goes on
a long business trip and leaves an Obliger spouse in charge
of three kids, that spouse would be wise to say something
like "You've been the solo parent, and I so appreciate everything you've done. I want you to take the weekend to get re-
energized—you do your own thing, and I'll take care of the
kids."

Because Obligers feel such pressure to meet external expectations, their spouses should be careful not to make offhand comments that might prove burdensome. A wife might
say in passing to her Obliger husband, "Maybe you should
coach Little League." Bam!

Dealing with an Obliger Child

In my observation, it's often difficult to tell if a child is an
Obliger or not. Upholders and Rebels are very extreme personalities and tend to show up fairly early, but children aren't
autonomous in the way that adults are, and adults control
children's lives to a very great extent—so it can be hard to
pinpoint Obliger characteristics.

When it is clear that a child is an Obliger, a parent can take that Tendency into account. Obliger children—like all Obligers—respond to accountability. If an Obliger child is supposed to practice the piano, it would be helpful to keep a chart of practice times, which the teacher or parents would review with the child. Gentle reminders help, too: "It's 4:00, time to practice." Or the teacher should explain, "I can tell if you've been practicing or not."

If an Obliger child wants to meet an inner expectation, parents should help him or her to figure out a system of external accountability to reinforce follow-through. One parent recalled, "My daughter wanted to teach our puppy a bunch of tricks. So I said, 'Great! Let's enter you in the 4-H dog show at the state fair this year.'"

However, beware of setting expectations too high— "Great! Let's enter you in the 4-H dog show. I'm sure you and Barnaby can win the blue ribbon!"—because the child may feel great pressure to meet them, which can lead to Obliger-rebellion.

Even more important, however, is to make sure that Obliger children don't work so hard to please others (including their parents) that they get overwhelmed, or that they lose sight of what makes them feel happy and fulfilled.

As in all contexts, when people ask for accountability, it's important that they get accountability. After I spoke at an event, a woman told me, "My daughter kept telling me, 'I want to take the GRE, I need to take a class.' And I kept answering, 'Nonsense, you can buy the GRE books and study on your own.' But now I realize, she's right, she should take the class."

People who ask for accountability know they need it.

Dealing with an Obliger Patient
or Health Client

Of the Four Tendencies, Obliger is the largest, which means that health-care professionals will be dealing with many, many Obligers. In general, Obligers benefit when a doctor, nurse, physical therapist, nutritionist, trainer, coach, or teacher monitors their progress. An exercise instructor, for example, might tell students that they'll get an email if they miss a class, or that he's keeping an attendance record, or that he'll be disappointed or annoyed if the Obliger doesn't show up.

I gave a talk about the Four Tendencies to the trainers at a popular New York City gym. Afterward, a trainer told me, "For accountability, we're told to use people's names when possible."

"That's a great idea," I said.

"But I realized something else I can do," she added. "When people leave, I've been saying, 'I'll be here next week.' Now I'm going to say, 'I'll see you here next week.' That way, people will feel like I'm expecting them."

"Brilliant!" I said.

As always, whenever people ask for accountability, it's wise to provide it, if possible. One Obliger recalled: "I told my dentist, 'Please hold me to my promise to floss. If I come back for my next exam and my mouth is in bad shape, call me on it!' She laughed but agreed to do it. I've been a nightly flosser ever since."

Each year, more devices, apps, and services come onto the market to help hold people accountable for health behaviors. While these can be extremely effective, it's important to match the accountability system to the actual Obliger. For some Obligers, it's enough to receive an email reminder to take a medication or to use a fitness tracker to monitor their daily exercise; for some Obligers, an app that imposed a fine would be useful. In the Better app, people can easily build accountability groups to create that sense of personal accountability. Most benefit from feeling accountable to an actual person.

Research shows that many people will pay extra for a commitment device. In fact, if I were a trainer, I'd tell people, "Our policy is that if you cancel within 24 hours of your session, we charge you anyway. If you prefer, we'll charge you triple if you cancel within 24 hours." Several Obligers have told me that they'd opt for the triple charge.

Often, Obligers can do something for others that they can't do for themselves, so they may be more likely to follow health-related instructions when they're reminded of the spillover benefits to others. And vice versa. One Obliger wrote:

> I'm six months pregnant, and for five months, I took my prenatal vitamins daily without fail, willing to do whatever possible for my baby's health. A month ago, I read an article explaining that the baby will never go without the necessary vitamins as it will rob the mother's stores, so the vitamins are more for the mother's health. Now that I connect the vitamins with my own health rather than the baby's, I'm lucky if I remember to take them every second day.

The people around Obligers should provide helpful accountability but should also avoid triggering Obliger-rebellion. They shouldn't push or nag too hard, or set goals that are too intimidating; instead, they should seek to help

Obligers feel encouraged, supported, and accountable, with reasonable bounds. Easier said than done.

Choosing a Career as an Obliger

Obligers can do just about anything well—if they have outer accountability and if they guard against Obliger-rebellion. When choosing a career path, Obligers should remember that they're more successful in work situations that supply outer accountability. One Obliger explained:

> I recently made a switch toward a more Obliger-friendly career. I started out in academia and did extremely well at the beginning, when I had an obligation to my Ph.D. supervisor to produce good research and write good papers. However, as I started moving toward career stages where my only obligation was toward myself and my own research, I found it increasingly difficult. I recently left academia for a teaching-only position, and I love it. Each day gives me opportunities to meet other people's expectations.

An Obliger boss explained, "Obliger fits perfectly with my organization's mission-driven and team-centered culture."

When making career decisions, Obligers must also guard against the impulse to meet others' expectations while disregarding their aspirations for themselves. Because this issue is at the core of the Obliger Tendency, Obligers must find ways to identify their inner desires and then develop external structures to hold themselves accountable. If they don't, they may find themselves very far down a career path that's wrong for them—which is when Obliger-rebellion often sets in.

While under the right circumstances Obligers can succeed in just about any career, many Obligers have told me that they believe that the Obliger perspective is practically a requirement of their field—in professions including corporate law, social work, private-wealth management, and medicine. "My team frequently pulls all-nighters to write code," one Obliger told me. "Sometimes a person comes along who says, 'Sorry, I'm not going to keep doing this.' And that person never lasts long."

After I spoke to a business group, a member came up to me to ask, "Now that I know the Tendencies, I'm going to hire only Obligers. I want employees who will meet work expectations, no matter what. Can you tell me how to screen for this during hiring?" I was somewhat taken aback. I don't think he had the best interests of those Obligers at heart.

SUMMARY: DEALING WITH
AN OBLIGER

They readily meet outer expectations but struggle to meet inner expectations

They put a high value on meeting commitments to others

They succeed when given accountability, with supervision, deadlines, monitoring, and other forms of accountability, such as the duty to be a good role model

They may have trouble setting limits on others' demands

They may have trouble delegating, because they feel that some expectations attach to them personally

They *must* have systems of external accountability in order to meet inner expectations

They may be exploited by people who take advantage of them, and because of that . . .

They may feel resentful or burned out, in which case . . .

They may need managers or others to alleviate expectations, or they may rebel

REBEL

"You can't make me, and neither can I"

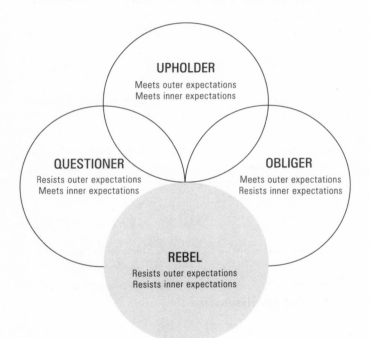

UPHOLDER
Meets outer expectations
Meets inner expectations

QUESTIONER
Resists outer expectations
Meets inner expectations

OBLIGER
Meets outer expectations
Resists inner expectations

REBEL
Resists outer expectations
Resists inner expectations

*"It's so hard when I have to, and
so easy when I want to."*

"MAY THE BRIDGES I
BURN LIGHT MY WAY."

"You're not the boss of me."

**"I do things only in my own
way—a blessing and a curse."**

"Ask forgiveness, not permission."

"I do what I want."

"BECAUSE I FEEL LIKE IT."

"Don't look, just leap."

"RULES MUST BE BROKEN.
EXCEPT, WOULD
THIS BE A RULE?"

"Freedom is my discipline."

"You can't make me, and neither can I."

"I'm happy to, when
I don't have to."

"YOU CAN'T SPELL 'REBEL' WITHOUT THE BE."

9

Understanding the Rebel

"It's so hard when I have to, and so easy when I want to"

Strengths (and Weaknesses) • Weaknesses (and Strengths) • Variations Within the Tendency • How Others Can Influence Rebels to Meet an Expectation • How Rebels Can Influence Themselves to Meet an Expectation • Why Rebels May Be Drawn to Lives of High Regulation

Every single day, all day long, each of us faces outer expectations and inner expectations—and we must decide, "Should I meet this expectation or resist it?"

For Rebels, the answer is always clear: Rebels resist *all* expectations, outer and inner alike. They want to do what they want to do, in their own way and in their own time, and if someone asks or tells them to do something, they resist. They don't even want to tell *themselves* what to do—they resist expectations imposed from within as vigorously as those imposed from without.

Rebels want to act from a sense of choice, freedom, and self-expression. Rebels wake up and think, "What do I feel like doing right now?" They resist control, even self-control, and often enjoy flouting rules, expectations, and conventions.

Rebels aren't persuaded by arguments such as "People are counting on you," "You've already paid for it," "I did this task, so will you do that task?" "I think this is really important, so let's agree that from now on we'll do it," "Things should be this way," "You have an appointment," "You said you'd do it," "This way is more efficient," "Someone else will be inconvenienced," "It's against the rules," "It's a tradition," "This is the deadline," or "It's rude."

They're much more apt to respond to being told "This will be fun," "This is what *you* want," "I'm feeling anxious about this, do you think you can do it?" "This feels really important to me, what do you think?" Rebels can do anything they *want* to do.

For Rebels, the ability to choose is so important that sometimes they make a choice—even when it's against their own self-interest or it's not what they prefer—just to reassure themselves that they *can* make that choice.

In my study, when people in the Four Tendencies were asked about how they stick to their good habits, Rebels were most likely to give the answer: "Usually I don't choose to bind myself in advance to a particular course of action."

Of the Four Tendencies, Rebel has the fewest members. It's a conspicuous group but a small one.

Strengths (and Weaknesses)

Rebels do something because they *choose* to do it, and so they're free from many of the pressures that the other Tendencies face.

Rebels tend to enjoy meeting challenges, when they can meet those challenges in their own way. A Rebel entrepreneur explained:

> As a Rebel, I get a boost from a challenge. "You think I can't start my own business? Watch me." Whenever I hear myself say "I can't . . ." or "I could never . . . ," I feel compelled to do it. I've amazed myself by the impossible things I've tackled just to prove to myself that I could. I think it could be dangerous and certainly manipulative to try to "dare" a Rebel into doing the right thing, but I will honestly say that it would probably work on me.

Rebels also take great pleasure in defying people's expectations. As a Rebel said, "Ever since someone told me I could get mugged on this greenway near our house, I've been more consistent in going for walks there. This may not be the best example of a healthy habit, but hey, it works." A Rebel who gave up alcohol explained, "People told me I could never quit drinking, and I love rubbing their faces in it and proving how wrong they were." In fact, in the survey I conducted, Rebels were more likely than the other Tendencies to agree with the statement "I don't mind breaking rules or violating convention—I often enjoy it."

When they're doing what they want, Rebels often drive themselves hard—especially if there's an element of "I'll show you." One Rebel wrote:

> The quiz said I was a Rebel, and at first I thought that couldn't be true. I'm a physique competitor (the bikini division of bodybuilding). I'm regimented about my diet and workouts. I thought, "No way would a Rebel live this way."

But this is something I do entirely because I want to, entirely the way I want to do it. I do it despite the fact that my husband doesn't understand it, my friends think it's weird, and it's a lot of work. I love watching people's faces when I tell them I'm a bodybuilder (I look slim, not bulky), or when I say I was a mechanic in the navy. I get a kick out of defying expectations. Rebel seems so obvious now.

Rebels easily defy customs and conventions. For instance, I've met several Rebel couples where the wife is the breadwinner, and when I read a *New York Times* article about patterns of marriage, housework, and earning, I thought about Rebels. The article reported that "wives who earn more [than their husbands] also do significantly more housework and child care than their husbands do, perhaps to make their husbands feel less threatened, the economists said." But maybe, it occurs to me, these men are Rebels who aren't bothered by the social convention that they should earn more than their wives—and, in the Rebel way, they don't feel much inclination to help out by doing boring, routine chores around the house, either. It's not a matter of masculinity, it's a matter of Tendency.

At times, the Rebel Tendency is enormously valuable to society. As one Questioner pointed out, "The Rebels' best asset is their voice of dissent. We shouldn't try to school it out of them, or corporate-culture it out, or shame it out. It's there to protect us all." Many "Rebels with a cause" use their Rebel spirit to support the principles and purposes they believe in. One Rebel explained, "I've always had the impulse to defy authority. I 'use my powers for good.' I've argued against rules, and sometimes even broken them deliberately, on behalf of others to whom they've been applied unfairly." Whenever I hear about people following an unconventional path—like the first woman to work on an oil rig—I think, hmmm, perhaps that's a Rebel.

One Rebel made an eloquent case for Rebeldom:

> A Rebel on a mission is a force of nature, a superstar. No need for checklists, for routines, rules, or habits to get things done. The need to find a cause, something to truly believe in and fight for, is vital. The inner belief is so strong, it will withstand any external pressure. A Rebel believes in his/her own uniqueness, and even superiority. There's certainly an aspect of arrogance. But if Rebels find the cause, then that's their master.

In a telling choice of vocabulary, a Rebel who took similar pride in being a Rebel referred to non-Rebels as Muggles.

Rebels place a very high value on authenticity and self-determination, and want their lives to be a true expression of their values. Others (especially Obligers) can find it very freeing to be with Rebels, because they're so in touch with what they want and have no trouble refusing obligations.

Rebels like to establish their own, often idiosyncratic, way of doing things. Right before a friend introduced me to someone she knew, she whispered, "Just so you know, he's a fist bumper." What? I wondered. But sure enough, when I held out my hand to shake, he held out his hand for a fist bump. He wasn't just going to shake hands like everyone else. A friend's Rebel son resisted applying to colleges until he decided to investigate international schools that no one else knew about; he enthusiastically applied once he'd found his own way.

Rebels often do better when there are no expectations at

all. One Rebel told me that she got her best grades during her final semester of high school, after she'd been admitted to a college, and her last year in college, when she already had a job lined up. Another Rebel said, "I'm writing a book, and I'm going to write the whole thing before I try to get a book contract, because the minute I have an editor and a deadline, I won't want to write."

As an Upholder, I've learned a tremendous amount from studying my "opposite," the Rebel. Rebels have shown me that *we're more free than we think*. If I refused to get up before 10:00 each morning, my family and my colleagues would adjust. If I decided I'd wear yoga pants and running shoes every day for the rest of my life, I could get away with that.

We're more free than we think.

Weaknesses (and Strengths)

While the Rebel Tendency carries many benefits, for Rebels and for the world, it's also true that Rebels often frustrate others (and themselves).

If a Rebel is asked or told to do something, the Rebel is very likely to resist, and this instinct can create problems—for spouses, health-care professionals, parents, teachers, office managers. The harder the push, the greater the Rebel pushback. I laughed when a Rebel friend told me, "No one can tell me to do anything. I recently got an email saying 'Please read' in the subject line, and I immediately deleted it."

Rebels resist just about anything they perceive to be an attempt at control—something as simple as a ringing telephone, a party invitation, or a standing meeting. This reaction happens even when they realize that their resistance is self-destructive, counterproductive, or contrary to their own desires. A Rebel told me, "Sugar makes me sick, but sometimes I think, 'I'm going to eat sugar,' because I refuse to accept the idea that I can't do something." Another Rebel wrote, "In high school, I started taking Ritalin for ADD, and my focus increased dramatically, but I thought, 'By what right does this drug control my personality? You think you can just pop in my mouth and make me do better in school—even though that's also exactly what I want?' So my focus increased, but my grades didn't."

One Rebel law student wrote:

> I live a fairly successful life but always in opposition to some kind of norm. Everyone expects me, as a law student, to work all night and live at the library; therefore I'm going to work in the afternoons at a coffee shop. At the school I go to, students are expected to go into corporate firms, because those are the best-paying jobs; therefore I'm going to specialize in constitutional law. However, in some situations my Rebel Tendency gets me in trouble. I'm currently neglecting to submit a time sheet that's months overdue, and I skip a lot of "mandatory" events or classes.

This self-description illustrates an important paradox: In their determination to be free, Rebels may end up being controlled. This student is specializing in constitutional law not because it interests him, but to flout the expectation that he specializes in corporate law. Rebellion is the opposite of compliance, but rebellion is not freedom.

I was reminded of this aspect of Rebeldom when a Rebel told me, "Peer pressure has the opposite of the intended result on me. If you try to convince me to do something, I automatically rebel and refuse to do it." He didn't see that he *was* responding to peer pressure—just in the opposite direction.

Rebels want to do tasks in their own time—and if someone pushes them to hurry, they're likely to resist and delay even more. The people around them may accuse them of being "procrastinators," but Rebels aren't necessarily reluctant to start work; they are refusing to be bossed around. The fact is, urging Rebels to do something will make them *less* likely to do it.

Of course, this pattern can be very frustrating for people around Rebels. One Obliger recalled her Rebel husband:

> I tended to step in on his behalf when he couldn't complete or start a task. I'd wait six months for a project to get done—then eventually feel that it was easier to do it myself. He would say that not everything could be done in my time frame. He once started a small home-improvement job that should've taken two weeks, and it took him more than a year. Each time I brought it up, he was annoyed. He didn't like my expectation, which he saw as controlling, and I didn't like the unfinished project.

As I read that, I thought, "Probably that job took a year *because* she kept reminding him to do it."

Rebels tend to resist committing to a schedule. Seeing an item on their calendar can make them feel trapped, and when they do make plans, they often cancel them at the last minute.

Rebels resist doing repetitive, boring tasks—such as taking out the garbage or filing expense reports—unless the consequences become serious enough. Many Rebels mention that they use automatic bill paying, and when they can afford it, they often pay to outsource routine obligations. Also, Rebels have learned that when they simply refuse to do something, other people often pick up the slack.

Of course, when we *must* do something, we do it—even Rebels. Often, however, when Rebels must do something, they find a Rebel way to get it done. I asked a Rebel friend how she managed to pay her bills on time, and without skipping a beat, she answered, "I pay them when I'm at the office, when I should be working." When another Rebel friend attends mandatory meetings, he does crossword puzzles on his iPad—conspicuously. The organization can make him come to the meeting, but they can't make him listen.

Even when Rebels acknowledge the reason for a restriction, they may find it hard to accept. One Rebel told me, "I've been married for five years, and I love my wife. But I have a problem with the idea of monogamy. I don't like people telling me what I can't do. I want to enjoy the full range of experience and achieve my complete potential, and that means being with more than one person." (He later divorced.)

Rebels often refuse to accept and be limited by a label—even one that's accurate. For instance, some Rebels move or change jobs frequently, to resist being trapped in one identity. Some Rebels will take positions in direct opposition to what they've said themselves, because they don't want to feel trapped in a particular view; they'll refuse to do a task that they said they'd do, because they don't want to be forced into action, even by their own former words. Rebels often don't care about reputation, or they may revel in being considered difficult or different (like many aspects of all the Tendencies, this can be both a strength and a weakness).

Rebels resist any system where someone else decides what they can do. I've noticed an interesting pattern: When applying to school, Rebels often apply to just *one school*. They know where they want to go, and they don't want an admissions committee deciding their future.

Although Rebels resist any expectations imposed on them, some Rebels feel quite comfortable imposing their expectations on others. As Samuel Johnson once remarked, with some asperity: "It has been observed, that they who most loudly clamour for liberty do not most liberally grant it." A Rebel wrote (presumably with a sense of humor about herself), "I want other people to do what I want, just like I want me to be able to do what I want."

When dealing with Rebels, it's crucial to accept that Rebelhood is a deep part of their nature; it's not a stage, it's not something that they will outgrow. A reader wrote me an email that struck me as quite poignant: "But surely Rebels eventually realize that we can't just do whatever we want—adults can't act that way." Adults *can* act that way, and Rebels *do* act that way. For better and for worse.

Variations Within the Tendency

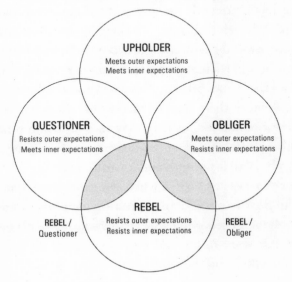

UPHOLDER
Meets outer expectations
Meets inner expectations

QUESTIONER
Resists outer expectations
Meets inner expectations

OBLIGER
Meets outer expectations
Resists inner expectations

REBEL / Questioner

REBEL
Resists outer expectations
Resists inner expectations

REBEL / Obliger

As with all the Tendencies, people of the Rebel Tendency overlap with two other Tendencies—Rebel overlaps with Questioner (both resist outer expectations) and Obliger (both resist inner expectations). Whether Rebels tip toward Questioner or Obliger greatly influences how they act.

REBEL/Questioners concentrate more on fulfilling their own desires than on resisting outer expectations; the Rebel spirit of resistance remains strong, but they're more focused on doing what they want than on defying other people. REBEL/Questioners have less trouble with resisting their own expectations for themselves; as one REBEL/Questioner remarked, "If I have nothing to rebel against, I do fine. No one cares if I go to the gym, so I go all the time. I love working for myself, but I struggle when working for others."

By contrast, REBEL/Obligers have a stronger dose of contrariness—of pushing back, of evading control. The Obliger and Rebel Tendencies both resist inner expectations, a state that fuels resentment and resistance. For this reason, REBEL/Obligers are more likely to insist "You can't make me!"—even if it's something the Rebel *wants* to do. For instance, in her essay in *The Atlantic* "I Refuse to Be a Grown-Up," REBEL/Obliger writer Elizabeth Wurtzel declares, "I do what I want. I don't do what other people want me to do. Sometimes I don't do things I want to do because someone else wants me to do them too badly."

For REBEL/Obligers, even if they want to do something, others' approval or encouragement may ignite their resistance to their own desires. One Rebel explained how his parents' loving attention actually interfered with his good habits: "If I try to form healthy habits for myself (wake up earlier, eat healthier) I find myself resisting and ultimately fail because I can feel my parents' silent approval—and so I don't want to do it!"

To sum up, REBEL/Questioners think, "I do whatever I choose," while REBEL/Obligers think, "I refuse to do what anyone tells me to do."

Of course, the Rebel Tendency mixes with other personality traits. A Rebel who's highly considerate of others will behave differently from a Rebel who's not considerate. An ambitious Rebel has a different life from a Rebel who doesn't care about career achievement. With some Rebels, their Rebelness is forceful and conspicuous; in other Rebels, it looks more like passive-aggressiveness—a quiet, nonconfrontational refusal to do what anyone else wants them to do.

Some Rebels love being Rebels. One Rebel declared:

> I've taken on things that other people thought were impossible. Rebels are game changers, revolutionaries, and out-of-the-box problem solvers. By being a Rebel, I empower others to step outside of their comfort zone and the established rules, about how things "should" be done.

However, while Obligers are the most likely to say they wished they belonged to a different Tendency, Rebels come next. Several people have told me that they call themselves a "Reluctant Rebel." They may feel isolated or frustrated; they may get embroiled in conflict. A Rebel explained,

> I envy the other Tendencies. I often feel like everyone around me is more content and better at "adulting" than I am. I get frustrated that I can't seem to make my big ideas come to fruition. I'm highly creative, and lately, I make most of my money through my photography and feel the pressure to take on more photography work and embrace this role. That thought literally makes me never want to pick up a camera again. I'm worried that if I focus in, I'd hate it.

When Rebels understand the Rebel pattern, they can manage its downsides to make their lives easier and happier.

How Others Can Influence Rebels to Meet an Expectation

Rebels do what they want, for their own reasons. If someone asks or tells them to do something, Rebels are likely to resist—so the people around Rebels must guard against accidentally igniting their spirit of opposition. Which is easier said than done.

A Rebel always wants to think "This is my idea"—and, in fact, many people have told me, "I manage Rebels by making them think that everything was their idea."

So how do we work most constructively with Rebels? In a nutshell, Rebels respond best to a sequence of *information, consequences, and choice.* We must give Rebels the information they need to make an informed decision; alert them to the consequences of actions they might take; then allow them to choose—with no lecturing, hovering, or hectoring.

- A parent might say, "If a person goes outside on a bright, sunny day, he gets a sunburn. A bad sunburn really hurts—skin can even blister and peel—and then the person is stuck inside while his friends are playing outside. Do you want to wear sunscreen lotion, or do you feel like wearing a hat and a long-sleeved T-shirt?"

- A teacher might say, "To graduate from high school, students have to complete a hundred service hours. Students who start as freshmen or sophomores have more choice about what projects they pick and when they do it. The longer students wait, the fewer choices they have. I've known seniors who've lost their spring break because they had to spend that time completing the service requirement. My door is open whenever you'd like to talk about choosing a service project."

- A spouse might say, "Because of kids' busy schedules these days, when families plan activities, they put things on the calendar far in advance. If you don't notify the Cub Scout families about when den meetings will be held until the week before you want to hold them, the boys might not attend. And our son will feel humiliated. You're the den leader, the schedule is up to you."

- A doctor might say, "Research shows that exercise really benefits people over the age of sixty. People who exercise are more likely to live independently and less likely to suffer debilitating falls and pain. If you're interested, this pamphlet has several suggestions for different kinds of exercise."

- A boss might say, "The client gave us a budget and a month's time to complete this project. If the client is pleased, this relationship might become permanent, which would mean more great projects and more money for all of us. Does this sound like something you want to tackle?"

Rebels do what they want—but if an action has unpleasant consequences, they may decide that they don't want to do it, after all. And even when they initially push back when someone says, "It's your choice, but have you considered . . . ?" they often end up incorporating that information into their decision making.

For information-consequences-choice to work, it's crucial that Rebels do indeed suffer unpleasant consequences—whether to a Rebel's health, reputation, or convenience. These unpleasant consequences can be painful to witness—and unfortunately, the consequences may affect others as well. However, if other people make problems go away, or do the Rebels' work for them, or cover for them, Rebels have no reason to act.

An Obliger friend and I were discussing this issue of consequences, and he told me, "I get it, absolutely. But the problem is, the consequences that fall on my Rebel wife also fall on *me*. If she doesn't pay the bill, my cable gets turned off. If she decides at the last minute that she doesn't want to go to that concert, my money gets wasted."

"Well," I said, trying not to sound harsh, "whatever it is, you need to find a way to frame the issue so that it appeals to her Rebel nature, or you have to let the negative consequences unfold."

In another conversation about a Rebel I know, a friend told me: "She was invited to this big benefit and she refused to RSVP. The organization called her repeatedly, saying, 'We need to get a final count for the caterer' and 'It's important for us to know your plans,' but she wouldn't answer. That night, she showed up, and she complained the whole time about how much she hated her table."

"See," I said, unable to pass up the chance to give a little lecture on the Four Tendencies, "the organization made the wrong arguments! They should've given information, consequences, and choice. 'If you respond now, you can choose where you sit, so you can sit with your friends. If you wait, those tables will fill up, and we'll assign you a seat with strangers. Let us know when you decide your plans.'"

Information, consequences, choice. Without lectures or micro-management or rescue.

Ironically, some Rebels' contrarian nature can make them easy to manipulate. Others can exploit their impulse to think, "You can't make me" or "I'll show you" or "Just watch me." A friend couldn't drag her Rebel daughter away from the television set, so she told her, "You've been under a lot of stress lately, you should relax. Stay home for a few days and watch TV." At which point her daughter stood up, turned off the TV, and walked out the door.

"I don't think you can finish the report by Friday," "I don't think you could give up sugar," or "I don't think you'll enjoy it" may all be good lines to use to trigger the Rebel spirit (though, true, some Rebels may see right through it). Remarking, "So I see you're not going to the gym today," might prompt the Rebel to say, "Oh yes, I am," while saying, "Don't you think you should go to the gym today?" might well prompt the answer of "I'm not going."

In fact, some psychotherapists use "paradoxical intervention" with patients, where they prescribe the very behavior that needs to be changed. There are various explanations for why this works, but I bet it works best when used with a Rebel. For example, if a child throws a tantrum every time she's told to make her bed, her parents might tell her, "Before you make your bed, take a few minutes and scream as loudly as you can."

One Rebel explained how she made sure she didn't fall into this trap of resistance. "As a Rebel, my first reaction when someone asks me to do something—or, worse, checks up on me—is 'No' or 'Leave me alone.' When that happens, I remind myself that I'm free to do it *even though* someone asked me to and wants me to do it—not doing something because someone asks is just as 'unfree' as doing it because someone asks."

Despite their impulse to resist if asked or told to do something, *Rebels may choose to do something out of love*—when they're acting from desire, not from obligation. If something is important to someone they love, they may *choose* to meet an expectation, to show love. But it's a choice. A Rebel teenager explained, "I'd plan to do something nice for my mom, some chore while she was out, and then as she'd leave the house, she'd tell me to do it. I'd think, 'No way! It was fun when I was going to do it as a surprise for you, Mom, but not now that it's an assignment.'"

The fact is, when doctors, parents, spouses, teachers, friends, or bosses push Rebels, they trigger Rebel resistance.

For instance, even a reward for good behavior—"If you finish your work, you can leave early"—is a mechanism of control that can have a bad effect on Rebels. Praise, or other attempts to encourage or motivate Rebels, can also backfire. One Rebel wrote:

I worked hard at a Couch to 5K program last summer. After I ran my first mile of my life, I posted it to Facebook. I got so much encouragement, so many people said "Keep it up!" and "See you at a 5K this fall!" It felt really good to get that praise at the time—but I never ran another mile again. I told myself it was because of a work trip, and the weather . . . but I was rebelling against all the expectations.

Another Rebel had a similar experience:

When I was in college and studying something I'd always wanted to study, I was doing quite well (95 average) when the professor called me into his office and told me I "could do better." From then on, my grades dropped. I felt like if I were to do well and get the 100 he was looking for, he would be winning somehow.

Rebels don't want to take direction from anyone, even to do something they enjoy. One reader wrote:

When I was first married, I couldn't understand why my husband didn't throw himself at me every time I put on my fancy lingerie. In time, it became a running joke with my-self: the way to guarantee a romance-free evening is to put on something black and lacy. Now I realize that my husband is such a Rebel, he doesn't even like to be "told" when to have sex. After almost twenty years of marriage, I've learned to keep my advances very low and casual, so he feels like it's his call, not mine.

For this reason, when a Rebel proposes to tackle some task, it's best not to interfere with a "better" plan:

If and when my Rebel husband is in the mood to do some-thing that benefits me, I'd better embrace it because it might not come around again! For example, in the old days if he said suddenly on a weeknight at 9:00, "I'm ready to clean out the garage," I might have said, "Oh, let's wait until the weekend when there's more time, when we can take stuff straight to Goodwill, I think we should get an early night, etc." Now I just say, "Great!"

The people around a Rebel may try to help, encourage, remind that Rebel to act. They become frustrated when the

Rebel refuses—but, in truth, it's their pushing that's slowing things down, because by pushing, they're creating resistance. One Rebel lamented:

> I was about to launch a job search until my husband (Obliger) started asking too many questions. He told me I wasn't trying hard enough. Now I've put off the search. I couldn't help but hold myself back, because I felt trapped and scrutinized. He says he wants to be more involved in my search and doesn't think I'm responsible enough to manage my own time. Everything would've been fine if he'd just left the subject alone.

Although Rebels don't like being told what to do and don't like being trapped into a schedule, sometimes compromise is possible; for instance, instead of trying to pin Rebels down to a specific slot on the calendar, let them choose within a wide time range. A coworker could say, "The boss is starting to give his usual boring lectures about how we need to submit a draft of next year's budget. So sometime next week, whenever you feel like it's a good time, let's review the budget for next year." Or a friend could say, "The next several months are going to be crazy, but I'm around this weekend. It would be fun to get together, so call me if you want to hang out."

Information, consequences, choice.

How Rebels Can Influence Themselves to Meet an Expectation

Rebels struggle to tell themselves what to do. While Rebels often frustrate other people, they may also frustrate themselves, because the imp of the perverse causes them to reject their own desires. An Obliger wrote to me:

> I asked my husband a few quiz questions on the sly (he wouldn't have taken it if I'd suggested it!), and he always answered Rebel. He doesn't want to be tied down, frequently changes his mind if you do get him to commit, and generally does the opposite of what's expected. He struggles with frustration over his inability to make himself do the things he wants in order to have a happy life. He hates that he doesn't go to the gym. He's pained that others view him as unreliable or undependable. I see so much good in his tenacity and steadfastness, but what do you do when you can't meet your own expectations for yourself?

Rebels seek to follow their own will, yet they're often undone by their own willfulness.

Following a schedule and making plans can feel like obligations to resist—even if the plan is something the Rebel *wants* to do. (To be sure, some Rebels love schedules, to-do lists, and the like, and they can follow this fairly un-Rebel-like behavior if that's what they *want* to do.)

Similarly, Rebels often get frustrated because they want to form habits—to exercise, to submit their freelancing invoices, to make sales calls—but they resist being locked in. Strategies used by other Tendencies to get things done often don't work for Rebels.

So what steps can a Rebel take? Rebels who resist plans, schedules, habits, and commitments can find ways to do things on their terms. The key thing for Rebels to remember: *They can do whatever they want to do.*

For instance, Rebels can meet expectations when those

expectations allow them to express their *identity*—to act like the kind of person they want to be. One Rebel explained:

> As a writer, if I sign up for a 30-day writing challenge, I doom myself. The worst thing to do is to post on my blog that I'm going to do something—I'll rebel against it. I tell myself that I want to be the kind of person who writes every day. I imagine forming a writing life by getting up and writing, how it will feel when I'm done with my words, and then I do it.

Because Rebels place great value on being true to themselves, they can embrace a habit if they view it as a way to express their *identity*. One Rebel explained it: "If a habit is part of who I am, then that habit isn't a chain holding me to the ground, it's permitting me to be authentic to myself." To meet financial goals, a Rebel could focus on his identity as a person who makes smart choices that give him long-term freedom. Another Rebel wrote: "Instead of expecting of myself to eat healthfully, exercise, floss, etc., I realized that I highly respect myself, and I want to take care of my body. That's part of my identity, and I naturally want to do these things."

Some imaginative Rebels play with their idea of their identity. One Rebel reported: "When I need to do repetitive chores, everything in me screams 'Noooo.' So I play a game I call 'As If.' I enact being somebody else or doing stuff while being filmed: e.g., I enact being a perfect butler, cook, interior designer, famous poet, cool scientist . . . sounds cheesy, but it works."

One Rebel combined the strategy of identity with the Rebel love of challenge: "To get things done, I trick my mind with a dare. I tell myself, 'I'm a Rebel who can stick to a routine and follow through.' This challenge excites me. It's rebellious to be a Rebel who can do disciplined things that you don't expect."

Similarly, Rebels can tie an activity to their deep values, by viewing it as an expression of who they are. "I got myself to commit to an exercise habit by signing up to run a marathon to raise money for a charity I really care about," a Rebel explained to me. "By tying running to my deep-seated urge to 'do something' for this particular cause, I was able to stick to it."

On the flip side, a Rebel recommended using the Rebel distaste for being trapped in a single identity—even the Rebel identity. He wrote, "I recognize my Rebel resistance and then (this is the important part) I reBEL against my REBel nature and choose the response that will help me meet my goal."

A Rebel identity can also be shaped by a negative—Rebels may choose to master habits because of who they *don't* want to be. "I'm not the kind of coach who keeps the kids waiting because I'm late to practice." A Rebel wrote, "My identity is 'responsible,' probably because my mother, the one I most rebelled against, always called me irresponsible."

Rebels use ingenious ways to avoid igniting their spirit of resistance—often by introducing an element of game, challenge, or choice. A Rebel said, "I interject challenge into the more strategic, long-term (but to me, boring) projects: 'I'll tame all of our company's paperwork around on-boarding freelancers by next Monday.'" Another Rebel turned the prospect of doing routine, scheduled tasks into a game:

> Instead of writing a to-do list, I write each task on a separate
> piece of paper. I fold up all the pieces and put them in a

bowl, then select one folded paper and do whatever task is written on it. I don't select another paper until that task is completed. This makes for a fun game of chance, and looking at the little folded papers feels less daunting than looking at a list of tasks.

Another Rebel was able to use a to-do list by making a simple change in vocabulary: " 'To-do' lists almost never get done by me, because as soon as I have to do something, it's the last thing I want to do. A 'could-do' list, however, reminds me that I can choose whether or not I complete the task."

In some cases, Rebels can reframe the situation so that instead of thinking, "This person expects me to do this task"— which triggers opposition—they think, "This person is doing what I want him to do, so I can get the result I want" or "This job is teaching me the skills I want." A Rebel friend explained to me, "My mortgage broker asked me to send her some information and I resisted until I thought, 'She works for me, she's refinancing my mortgage, so I have more money to spend, not to pour into the pockets of some big bank.' And then I was able to send the information."

The Rebel dislike of constraint can be a positive force, enabling Rebels to resist cigarette smoking, junk food, alcohol, technology, or anything else that starts to feel addictive or confining or controlling. One Rebel wrote:

When I was trying to follow a diet, I'd sometimes think, "I can't do what I want," and that would make me rebel against it. Now I think the reverse: "I can do whatever I want, and what I want is to eat this new way."

I view unhealthy food as something corporations try to push on us. They load it with fat and salt and sugar to try to get us to eat their unnutritional, chemical-ridden crap. They try to hook us, to make us crave it, to make us slaves to it. Well, you can take your expensive, worthless junk and shove it! That's what I think of all cookies, crackers, chips, white flour, refined sugar, and even hippie-dippie products trying to pose as healthy alternatives. Rebel enough for you?

I don't feel deprived because as a Rebel, I break my own rules randomly and have treats when I want them. It's just that most of the time I rebel against the unhealthy food industry.

Rebels dislike being tied to a schedule, so they do better when they do what they want, when they want—without any expectations that might trigger resistance. For instance, instead of putting exercise reminders in a smartphone—which could trigger resistance—a Rebel might keep schedules for all the exercise classes in the neighborhood and, when the mood strikes, choose whatever class that sounds appealing.

Rebels can do whatever they want to do, and they'll often remind themselves of why they want to avoid negative consequences. A Rebel told me, "I file my taxes on time because hassling with the IRS is more trouble than it's worth, which I learned from experience. I use my turn signals, not because I'm obeying traffic laws, but because I don't want to get hit by some idiot."

Some Rebels use negative consequences as a way to force themselves to act. I heard of one ambitious Rebel writer who kept herself prolific by giving away money as fast as she earned it. She knew that if she didn't have to write to make money, she wouldn't be able to make herself write.

When Rebels understand the Rebel Tendency, they can

harness the power of their Tendency to help them do everything they want to do.

Why Rebels May Be Drawn to Lives
of High Regulation

The Rebel Tendency contains surprising paradoxes. For instance, some Rebels gravitate to institutions with many expectations and rules, such as the military, the police, large
corporations, and religious communities.

For some Rebels, this reflects a deep need for purpose. One
Rebel explained: "I think a Rebel desires to be in the military
or the clergy because it offers a sense of purpose in the midst
of the daily junk. A Rebel in an office (like me) feels trapped
in a cage." Another Rebel agreed: "You find Rebels among
ministers and the military because they've found something
big enough to deserve all their energy and devotion."

Also, many Rebels get their energy and direction from
pushing back, and highly regulated environments supply
Rebels with rules to ignore, limitations to exceed, conventions
to violate. One Rebel wrote:

> As a former member of the Marine Corps, I agree that
> there's a high incidence of Rebels in the military. My obser-
> vation, as a Rebel myself, is that it's true because often Rebels
> can create quite a mess for themselves because they refuse to
> adhere to rules of society and may be given the choice of jail
> or the military (two people close to me were in this scenario).
> Second, the military provides a plethora of rules to follow,
> which allows for numerous options for breaking these rules.
> This was how I survived the rigidity of the Marines. Many

rules are not life-threatening, so I broke a lot of them. Even still, I had a great career and earned many awards.

Working in positions that have a lot of structure may suit some Rebels who find that too much freedom causes them to founder. As one Rebel put it, "I war against the Establishment, but I want it to be there so that I have something to war against."

In studying the Rebel attraction to high regulation, I was struck by the example of Thomas Merton. Merton was a Trappist monk whose writings were very influential in the 1950s and 1960s; in 2015, he was named by Pope Francis as an American who provides inspiration to the world today. Over and over, in his extensive writing, Merton expresses the Rebel perspective: the impulse of opposition, the craving for freedom, the determination to do things his own way.

For Rebels, freedom is the paramount value, and for Merton, freedom comes from the total surrender to God's will; a surrender that promises an escape from relentless rebellion and from the ego, with its demands, noise, and pain.

In 1941, Merton became a Trappist monk at the Abbey of Gethsemani in Kentucky, but he became a Trappist in his own way. Although Trappists follow a strict schedule of communal work, Merton persuaded the abbot to let him establish a "hermitage," and once Merton moved to that hermitage, he was free from almost all monastic obligations and communal labor—and not only that, his "hermitage" became the place where he met with scores of visitors, free from any supervision.

Merton's most spectacular rebellion came in 1966, when, after an operation, he fell in love with a student nurse, M. Merton didn't hesitate to break the rules. He and M. had many "illegal" visits, letters, and phone calls, and Merton dragged his friends into the deception by asking them to help him arrange meetings. It seemed clear to Merton that God approved of whatever Merton wanted to do.

The Rebel Tendency is one of power and paradox.

SUMMARY: REBEL

LIKELY STRENGTHS:

Independent-minded

Able to think outside the box

Unswayed by conventional wisdom

Willing to go his or her own way, to buck social conventions

In touch with his or her authentic desires

Spontaneous

POSSIBLE WEAKNESSES:

Likely to resist when asked or told to do something

Uncooperative

Inconsiderate

Has trouble accomplishing tasks that need to be done
consistently, the same way, every time

Acts as though ordinary rules don't apply

Restless; may find it difficult to settle down
in a job, relationship, city

Struggles with routines and planning

May be indifferent to reputation

10

Dealing with a Rebel

"You're not the boss of me"

Work • Spouse • Child • Health Client • Choosing a
Career

Dealing with a Rebel at Work

Rebels can bring great strengths to work: their willingness to
break with convention, their ability to think outside the box,
their connection to their authentic interests and desires.

A Rebel sent me this image, with a great Rebel motto:

> If I had to describe myself
> using only one word
> it would be
> "doesn't follow directions."

Rebels thrive at work—when work aligns with their
aims.

Rebels can be very productive, but usually only if they're
allowed to do their work in their own way. The less bossing

and supervision they get, the better—though it's true, paradoxically, that some Rebels do need structure to ignore and push against.

Many Rebels respond well to a challenge or to a dare, and they thrive in an environment where they do their work their way. One Rebel explained:

> In my first job out of college, I worked at a big consulting firm. I had a fantastic boss. He gave me a tough project and said, "Look, here's a big problem. I don't know how to solve it, you run with it. Come back to me in three months with an answer. Call me if anything gets in your way." I did my best work under those conditions. I loved it. But then he left, and I got a new boss who wanted to micro-manage me. I ended up quitting and starting my own company.

Note that this boss's hands-off approach, while very effective for a Rebel, might not work for an Obliger.

While Rebels love a challenge, they often struggle with mundane, repetitive tasks—which may or may not be a big deal, depending on the workplace. A Rebel described herself: "To overcome my utter failure at routine tasks, I work my tail off on things that I do like—big, interesting challenges. I'm pretty successful, but I think I should be more successful given how hard I work. A lot of my work is making up for shortcomings in routine areas." Perhaps she and her boss could reassign some of those routine tasks, which don't get done anyway, so the Rebel can focus on big challenges.

Although Rebels generally don't take orders or directions well, some Rebels work well with others when they themselves are in charge. As one Rebel explained, "I want everyone to do things my way, from my employees to my children. It's chaotic being a Rebel, and not wanting to conform to anything, so I choose employees who can cooperate with me."

A Rebel friend who's a respected professor told me, "Academia attracts Rebels."

"But what about getting tenure?" I asked.

"You have to publish to get tenure, but you choose what to do—one book, two books, lots of articles. Once you have tenure, you don't have to do anything except teach your classes, and you have a lot of freedom about how to do that. The dean doesn't say, 'You'd better produce, it's been ten years since your last book'—even if that's what he's thinking. I write because I want to write, not because someone is making me."

As bosses, Rebels can be exciting, creative leaders who possess the determination and drive to pursue their vision. And they can also be very hard to work for.

A Questioner wrote:

When I realized my former boss was a Rebel, I finally understood behavior that I, as a Questioner, couldn't understand. She'd receive a request from her boss and find fault in what she was asked to do, even if it was something she'd been planning to do. We'd set up an office process, and she'd discard it a week later.

As a Questioner, it was very uncomfortable to work for a Rebel. I didn't understand why she made the choices she made, or why she couldn't stick to a decision. There never seemed to be any logical reasoning behind her decisions or assignments.

At work with Rebels, it's helpful to provide information, frankly present possible consequences, and allow them to choose how to act. Information-consequences-choice: "The weekly staff meeting is where we make many important decisions and where we divide up the work. If you skip the meeting, you won't have a voice in the direction of this company, and you might get stuck on less desirable assignments."

A Rebel who wants to be seen as a strong leader, a powerful visionary, or a supportive boss will choose to act in harmony with that identity. "When you attend the monthly meetings, the staff feels like you're interested in hearing their ideas and frustrations. When you don't go, you seem unapproachable, like you don't care about their views."

Rebels often want to start their own businesses or work freelance because they want to do their own work, in their own way, on their own schedule, with no one telling them what to do. But then they often struggle because they don't want to tell *themselves* what to do. They can't stand deadlines; they resist doing detailed or repetitive work; they don't want to be locked into a schedule.

For this reason, Rebel entrepreneurs often pair up with someone—usually an Obliger—who ensures that essential tasks get done. I talked to a Rebel who had launched a successful Internet site: "I supply the vision, I'm the voice of the brand, I generate the ideas for where we should go next. Some days I go into the office, some days I don't. My cofounder deals with advertisers, manages the staff, and oversees the financial side."

Just as they often pair with Obligers, Rebels often pair with family members as work partners—perhaps because a relative has more understanding, experience, and tolerance for the Rebel.

Dealing with a Rebel Spouse—and the Pattern of the Rebel/Obliger Couple

Because of the challenges of dealing with a Rebel sweetheart, more than one person has asked me, "Are Rebels less likely to be in a long-term relationship?" The representative sample reveals that Rebels are just as likely as any of the Tendencies to live with a spouse or long-term partner.

Recognizing that someone is a Rebel makes the pattern of his or her behavior much clearer. A college friend told me, "Knowing that my husband is a Rebel makes me feel better about our relationship. Now I don't take it personally when I say, 'Let's do this,' and he says, 'I'll never do that.' It's not a reflection of how he feels about me or the health of our marriage. It's just the way he is, with everyone."

For Rebels, as for all of us, consequences can sometimes be dire enough to goad them into action. One Upholder described how her Rebel husband, when faced with a divorce, changed his behavior—out of love:

> The truth is, at first I did do all the work. The marriage fell apart within a year. But my husband dragged me to marriage counseling, and we have learned to respect each other's differences.
>
> As an Upholder, I have a lot of motivations. But my Rebel husband is motivated by only one thing: LOVE. He does things out of love, and love only. He has figured out the things that matter to me, and he works hard to support me in them because he loves me. Our particular combination of personalities has given us a unique lifestyle. I own a successful business and my husband is the primary caretaker for our children.

The key point for the spouse of a Rebel? *The more that's asked, the more the Rebel will resist.* As one spouse of a Rebel told me, "It has taken me twenty years to realize that the less I ask for, the more I get."

A striking pattern among Rebels is that *if a Rebel is in a successful long-term relationship, at home or at work, that Rebel is usually paired with an Obliger.*

Few Upholders or Questioners welcome a Rebel's behavior. The Upholder thinks the Rebel is impulsive and irresponsible, and the Rebel thinks the Upholder is rigid; the Questioner thinks the Rebel is driven by impulse, and the Rebel thinks the Questioner spends too much time analyzing.

Obligers, much more than Upholders or Questioners, take satisfaction from Rebel actions and can benefit from the Rebel perspective.

Unlike Upholders and Questioners, who are unsettled by the Rebel's expectation-rejecting behavior, Obligers may benefit from and enjoy (at least sometimes) the Rebel's refusal to truckle to outward expectations. For an Obliger, who feels tremendous pressure to meet outer expectations, it's a relief to be with someone who happily disregards them. An Obliger married to a Rebel recalled, "My husband got an all-expenses-paid trip to a writers' event in an exotic place. We went, and they wanted us to attend panels, go to cocktail parties, etc. I said, 'Gosh, they invited us, and they're paying for it all, we have to do these things.' He said, 'No way, we don't have to do any of it.' And we didn't do anything we didn't want to do."

Another Obliger (tipping to Rebel) explained why she liked the company of Rebels:

> We Obligers do have that rebellious streak—like I love non-traditional hair colors. That's why we love Rebels. Rebels tell

us it's okay to indulge that rebellious nature, and that gives Obligers the freedom from some obligations. My husband and best friend are Rebels. They make life more fun and think my "weird" style is cool. Plus they remind me when it's time to take care of myself before I hit burnout. Whereas Questioners and Upholders (my brother and stepfather) just keep asking why I took on so many responsibilities if I "couldn't handle them."

In fact, Rebels may save Obligers from falling into Obliger-rebellion, because a Rebel will encourage an Obliger to resist an outer expectation. As one Obliger put it, "Living with a Rebel can sometimes be challenging, but the one word he understands is no. For him, it's normal to not feel like doing something, and he doesn't expect me to say yes to everything. Since I feel that *not obliging* is often harder than *obliging*, this gives me more space to be myself." This permission may act as a relief valve to the pressure of expectations that the Obligers feel.

On the Rebel side of the Rebel/Obliger pairing, an Obliger makes it easier for the Rebel to ignore everyday expectations—because the Obliger picks up the Rebel's slack. One Rebel wrote, "I'd say my husband is a great partner who makes my life smoother by doing the chores of daily life, but hopefully he'd say that I help him live in the moment and enjoy the journey." The marriage works if both people agree that this is an acceptable trade-off.

An Obliger friend told me, "Where we live, we need car toll tags. I got my Rebel husband a toll tag, put it on the counter for him to put in his car, he 'lost' it, and now he has a huge stack of fines for not paying his toll."

"Aren't you annoyed," I asked, "that as a family, you've wasted all that money?"

"No, he knows that I'll contact the authorities and tell them that we did have the toll tag, but it was defective, and get the fine excused, but still, that's work that I'm going to have to do—because he hates the idea of having to pay the toll."

As an Upholder, I must say, I was *staggered* by this story.

Another Obliger with a Rebel spouse recalled, "Before getting married, I visited a friend's house, and stuck to the fridge was a list of 'His' and 'Hers' chores. I was appalled, and I thought, 'I'd never keep a list like that. That's not the kind of score-keeping marriage I want.' For me, harmony is the most important thing. I'd rather do more work than worry about keeping track of what the other person is doing."

To me, as an Upholder, her desired arrangement seems unfair. I'd feel resentful if Jamie imposed expectations on me without assuming any himself. But perhaps to others I might seem like the scorekeeper that this Obliger didn't want to be.

A friend said, somewhat bitterly, "Rebels are the people we all take care of." And that's the paradoxical aspect to this pattern: The Rebels become dependent. Their freedom from the mundane responsibilities of life is often possible because someone else handles the duties of daily existence for them.

Similarly, while refusing to commit to plans makes Rebels feel free, their behavior often allows others to set the agenda. One Rebel explained, "I have the most fun when my husband (who has the itinerary planned out) doesn't tell me the plan ahead of time. He says, 'This is what's happening, if you want to join in for any or all of it.' We just flow from one activity to the next, and it's fun and feels spontaneous." Well, it feels spontaneous to *her,* and she feels as if she's making her own choices—but someone else is setting the itinerary.

When Rebels are paired with Questioners or Upholders, the relationship may take much more work. A Questioner with a Rebel husband and child wrote:

> I get why the Rebel spirit might have been great during the French Resistance. But we're not living during the French Resistance now. I regret that I married a Rebel. He was far more agreeable to my requests when we were dating. Once we got married, that stopped. We can try to make the best of it, but it's just way harder than it could be had I married, say, an Obliger. And I drive him crazy with all my questions.

Not all such pairings are this difficult. For instance, at dinner, I sat next to an Upholder husband married to a Rebel. When I asked him—in more delicate terms—how he put up with it, he explained, "It works because my wife is a highly considerate, loving person." "Interesting," I thought. A good example of how a person's Tendency is just one aspect of their personality. "If I ask her to do something," he continued, "her immediate response is to say no. But after a week or so, she'll propose her own solution that takes my view into account."

"Like what?"

"For instance, she proposed some porch furniture, and I said I thought it might look cluttered. She said, 'No, you're wrong, it will be fine'—but a week later, she showed me her new plan, and it was much less cluttered."

"Right." I nodded. "Has she ever refused to do something, where you considered it a big problem?"

"Oh, sure. Like when we got married, she didn't write thank-you notes. That was a big issue."

"Couldn't you have written the notes?" I asked.

"I would have! But by the time I realized that this was an

issue, we'd opened a bunch of gifts without keeping track of who gave us what, and it was too late." He sighed. "I can still get worked up, thinking about it."

Another Upholder married to a Rebel explained the dynamics of their marriage:

> My husband and I met in college, and our Tendencies were clear from the start; in college, I excelled, he almost flunked out. Although my husband is incredibly intelligent, when he had an assignment he didn't like, he chose to answer different questions than the ones posed by the instructor. He learned on his own terms, but this often resulted in a failing grade. My husband also attended college as a nontraditional student (he started at 24) because he does things on his own timeline. I'm a dedicated rule follower with two graduate degrees.
>
> It took me a while to understand that my husband will frequently do the opposite of what I recommend or ask. Although many people might find these differences difficult, I appreciate my husband's independence.
>
> My husband's Rebel Tendency has helped us follow a more unconventional lifestyle. Since I'm the more career-oriented, he has moved several times to follow my career, and I'm currently the breadwinner. We don't have any children by choice. My husband is working on writing a novel from home. He financially (and emotionally) supported me while I completed my M.A. and Ph.D., and he quit as soon as possible to pursue his writing. We share domestic tasks and each cook for ourselves.
>
> I've come to appreciate that his Rebel Tendency means that I'm off the hook when it comes to his life choices (although it can be difficult when those life choices overlap

with mine) because I literally cannot force him to do anything.

As with all relationship combinations, success comes when we can focus on the positive aspects of our sweetheart.

Dealing with a Rebel Child

Unprompted, many Rebels have told me about the specific moment when they realized, as young children, that no one could make them do anything. "I was sitting on the floor and my mother was trying to make me put on my shoes," wrote one Rebel. "And I thought, 'She can't make me!' and I refused. I sat there for two hours."

Rebel children can be a challenge. When they're asked or told to do something, they tend to resist. They want to choose their own way; they don't want others to set expectations. A friend said, "I told my Rebel daughter that I would tuck her in 'in five minutes.' She responded, 'How about four?'"

The fact is, though parents, teachers, and coaches often want to push Rebels, that's a very counterproductive strategy. A fifteen-year-old Rebel explained:

> I lived with my liberal, freedom-giving mom for twelve years until I moved in with my conservative, restrictive, discipline-oriented Upholder dad. With my dad, if I do something he needs, he gets triumphant, and says something like "If only you did that more often." Whenever he's not like this, we have a great relationship, but when he asks me to do something, I resist. He doesn't understand how I work, and he thinks I'm lazy and disrespectful.

Sadly, this father hasn't figured out that telling a Rebel child what to do doesn't work. It's possible to *make* a child do something, of course, by establishing consequences that are sufficiently dire—but that's very difficult to enforce over the long run.

So what does work? The same formula that works with adults: information, consequences, choice—with no nagging or badgering.

This is tough. It can feel scary to allow Rebel children to do what they want—but since prodding them to follow a certain course so often backfires, it's more effective to trust to their own judgment (as risky as that might seem).

One parent of a Rebel explained, "The best way to wrangle the Rebel child is to give the kid the information to make a decision, present the issue as a question that he alone can answer, and let him make a decision and act without telling you. Let him make a decision without an audience. Audiences = expectations. If he thinks you're not watching, he won't need to rebel against your expectations."

One serious Rebel issue? A child who wants to drop out of school. I heard from one member of a family that decided to accommodate a child's Rebelness:

My sister Lynne is clearly a Rebel. She's struggled since kindergarten, never due to lack of intelligence. Throughout high school, she's talked about dropping out. This summer, it looked like it was finally going to happen (with only one year left to go).

Before my parents sat down to talk to her about it, I'd suggested to my mom that she let Lynne drop out. I explained Lynne's Rebel Tendency and how she'd find a way to do what she wanted. My mom reluctantly agreed.

A few weeks go by, and Lynne starts talking about finishing high school online, instead of dropping out. Today, she told me she's going back to school. They reworked her schedule to suit her needs better.

Without a doubt, my parents letting Lynne make her own decisions brought this result. She feels in control and like it's her decision (which it is). I can't help but wonder what would've happened if they'd pushed her to stay in school.

Along the same lines, I heard from a teacher:

I'm a teacher at our local county jail, mostly GED and high school diploma courses. Recently I had a student who was getting in her own way—arguing with the guards and not completing assignments. I believed her when she said that she really wanted to get her GED—yet she wasn't making progress.

It dawned on me that she is a Rebel. I shared your theory with her, and it really helped her see herself in a new, more positive way. I stopped asking her to do homework and let her decide each day how she wanted to study: computer software, group lesson, independently, or not at all. As I write this, she has passed five of the five tests, and thus completed her high school equivalency.

Rebels can do whatever they *want* to do.

Because Rebel children are likely to resist if an adult asks or tells them to do something, it's very important to pay attention to language and to avoid anything that smacks of an order. To a parent, saying, "Honey, tell Aunt Jane what a nice time you had" may not seem like a command—but it is. The Rebel child may have intended to say something polite—but no longer. Instead, in the car on the way to Aunt Jane's house, a parent could remark, "Even though it's not much fun to visit Aunt Jane, you remember to thank her every time we see her. You show real thoughtfulness in the way you speak to her." Then let the child decide how to behave.

A music teacher explained how she tailored her approach to a Rebel student:

> I'd tried to help one Rebel student to become a leader rather than a "disrupter." So I'd ask him to do things, like pass out supplies, help the person next to him. I could see he wanted and liked to be in charge . . . so why was he not jumping at the chance to lead and help his neighbors? I learned that as a Rebel, he refuses because he wants leading and helping to be his decision, not mine. So I told the class, "Show me your part of the song and hand movements, all of you at the same time. I want to see who's doing a good job, so I can find a leader." Now, he has a choice: Is he going to try hard, or is he going to shy away? Well, he tried really hard. So I asked him, "Do you want to be leader for your section?" I didn't tell him, I asked him. He said yes. Man oh man was he excited to lead that section.

To try to channel a Rebel child's energies and interests, it's helpful to point out how much he or she enjoys an activity, so the child may choose to keep doing it. "Wow, seems like you like writing for the newspaper, it's fun to see your name in print and to hang out with everyone else who works on the paper." "It feels good to see your name on the list for the honor society."

Parents and teachers can help Rebels spot the reasons they might want to meet an expectation. For example: "Kids who get good grades this semester will qualify for the class trip to the White House next spring." One Rebel music teacher explained, "To motivate Rebel students, I emphasize the incredible opportunities that they might have if they play well. That's what worked for me . . . the chance to be admired!"

Rebels respond much better when an action is framed in terms of choice, freedom, and self-expression instead of constraint and duty. "When you want to learn to ride a bike, you can, and then you can ride off with your friends on fun adventures." Not, "Your friends will make fun of you if you can't ride a bike."

With Rebels, it's crucial to be frank about the consequences of not meeting an expectation—and to allow them to experience those consequences. But this can be painful, for both parent and child. One Rebel explained:

> As a Rebel myself, I'd say this: Rebels learn best by suffering the consequences of their decisions. I can assure you that I pay my bills on time and that everything in my house is in working order. If you're parenting a Rebel child, you may have to suffer along with them while they learn the consequences of their decisions. But the quicker you allow this to happen, the sooner they will learn what they can get away with—and what they can't.

Also, Rebels are powerfully motivated by identity, so it can be helpful to tie an action to an identity that the child values. A Rebel recalled:

> The most effective approach is to give Rebels a choice that resonates with their identity. For example, punctuality was a source of tension between my mother and me for years.

She would nag, gently remind, yell—nothing helped. Finally, one day she said, "Look, right now, I feel like I can't trust or rely on you. I also feel like when you keep me waiting, you're telling me that your time is more important than mine. If that's who you want to be—someone that others can't rely on and who makes them feel unimportant, fine. Or, you can be someone that people can trust, rely on, and who makes others feel valued. It's your choice." It was like a switch flipped instantly. Because she gave me a choice— and I immediately knew what resonated with my sense of authentic self. Then it became easy.

Also, if something's enjoyable, a Rebel is far more likely to do it. With a Rebel child (and this is true of most children, of course), it can help to make an activity more fun. "To get my son to brush his teeth," one father recalled, "we'd make up games. He'd pretend to be a vet cleaning the teeth of a bear, or a mechanic washing off an engine." A Rebel child might enjoy a challenge: "Bet you can't get ready in less than two minutes, can you beat your old record?"

One helpful example of dealing with a Rebel child appears in one of my favorite books, Laura Ingalls Wilder's *These Happy Golden Years*. Just sixteen years old, Laura (a Questioner, by the way) is teaching school, and her student Clarence is a Rebel who refuses to study. He can't stand to be told that he must do schoolwork, and he refuses, even though he's a smart boy who wants to learn.

When Laura asks her parents for advice, Ma observes, "Better not try to make him do anything, because you can't." So Laura changes her approach. After Laura gives the other students their assignments, she tells him, "This doesn't mean you, Clarence; it would make your lesson far too long. . . .

How much do you think you can learn? Would three [pages] be too much?"

In this way, she does two things. First, she leaves the choice to Clarence and gives him freedom. Second, she gives him the kind of challenge that Rebels often respond to. When she suggests that he can't master three pages, and when the other students start pulling ahead of him, he thinks, "I'll show her." Within a week, Clarence has caught up to the rest of his class.

It's crucial to remember that for Rebels, they must feel that they're doing what they want, not what others want. A Rebel wrote, "If you tell me to do something, I feel like your prisoner. But if you tell me, 'Here are four possibilities, decide for yourself,' then it's more likely that I'll do one."

I've noticed that Rebel children seem to have unusually close relationships with grandparents—maybe with grandparents, they find the satisfaction of a close family bond, with fewer expectations.

Because they understand the Rebel perspective, Rebels may find it easier to raise a Rebel child. One Rebel mother wrote, "My four-year-old daughter is a Rebel as well. She loves choices and getting to make her own decisions, not just for herself but for all of us. And I totally get it, so I let her pick out her own clothes, pick out my clothes, choose sleep over getting to preschool on time, have spaghetti for breakfast and eggs for dinner." Of course, this pairing has its own challenges. A Rebel friend told me with a sigh, "When we're at a restaurant, I don't want to tell my son to stop blowing mustard through the straw onto the table. I want to do it, too."

As always, when we recognize a Tendency, we can communicate more effectively with a particular person. No matter how much love we feel, if we don't understand how to reach someone, our most well-intentioned words and actions can go astray.

Dealing with a Rebel Patient or Health Client

The Rebel Tendency can contribute to real health issues.

Because Rebels will resist if told to do something, many strategies that work well on Upholders, Questioners, or Obligers may be *counterproductive* for a Rebel. This pattern can be very frustrating for people trying to help Rebels with health issues; well-intentioned advice, encouragement, reminders, and admonitions may push Rebels into doing the opposite of what would be good for them. Even the medical condition itself can seem like something to resist. For instance, one Rebel explained:

> I'm a type 1 diabetic, and I have a hard time dealing with how this health problem controls how I feel and what I do. I know that I should view looking after myself as "taking control over my diabetes" instead of vice versa, but I can't seem to grasp that. I hardly ever check my blood sugar, I take fast-acting insulin sporadically—I don't like to schedule meals!—and I haven't seen my endocrinologist in years, so I actually don't even know what my A1C is.

Rebels can't stand the idea of "following doctor's orders." In fact, if a doctor praises a Rebel by saying, "You're doing great, you're following my directions exactly," the Rebel might immediately stop, in order to demonstrate freedom.

Rebels do better when they're reminded that any action

is their choice. Instead of telling a Rebel, "You must do X," a doctor might suggest, "It's up to you, of course, but X is often effective." "Have you considered trying X?" "What would you think about X?" "Some people have found that X works for them," or "Some ideas for you to consider include X, Y, and Z."

Rebels resist even the rules that they try to impose on themselves. One Rebel college student explained, "I'm struggling with extra weight, but the minute I make a rule about eating at night, I start eating more at night. Or I say I'll give up bread and then I go buy a beautiful loaf of sourdough." Another Rebel figured out a clever way to work around this kind of self-resistance: "If I want to eat healthy, I'll eat the chocolate or the 'bad' thing first thing. I show myself, 'I won the war, I do what I want!' And the rest of the day, I feel free from rebelling against me telling me what to do."

To help a Rebel, as always, it's most effective to provide information, consequences, and choice. As one Upholder doctor reported:

I'm a family physician, and I had a patient who was very resistant to my recommendations to help with weight loss and to treat pre-diabetes/insulin resistance. As I talked to her, "Rebel" popped into my head. I switched gears and made a list of suggestions she could try "if she wanted to," rather than using the more directive style that I find works best with most people. This patient did come back for a later visit, and she'd taken one of my suggestions. Her weight was down, and she was feeling much better. I don't think the result would have been the same had I been directive. That approach works with the Upholders and Obligers, and also Questioners, because I always give a detailed explanation of my recommendations. But for the Rebel, that strategy just doesn't work.

Rebels may benefit from information like knowing their daily weight or the number of steps they're taking—and it's more helpful to frame monitoring efforts as "You might find it interesting and useful to know how much exercise you're getting," rather than "You need to take 10,000 steps every day, so you should wear this activity tracker."

An appeal to choice, freedom, and pleasure works with Rebels: This drug/diet/exercise routine/daily habit will make you feel better, give you more energy, take away pain, prove interesting, improve performance, enhance your sex life, give you the life you want. A nutritionist could say, "One client found that when he gave up sugar, he had more stamina, and his tennis game improved." Instead of telling a Rebel what to do, the nutritionist is giving information to help the Rebel decide what to do. One Rebel recalled:

> My favorite personal trainer always told me, "Maybe you just want to try it for a week, and if you don't like it, don't do it anymore." No pressure, no guilt, no real rules, just discover yourself—and always, always against the mainstream. I don't stick to programs very well. All those 30-day things feel so restricted. If I do choose to do these programs, I need to break one of the rules.

It's also possible to offer help: "Would it make your life easier if I organized the weekly pills?" "Would you enjoy walking more if I came with you?"

I got an email from someone desperate to push her Rebel husband to quit smoking. No surprise, her constant admonishments weren't working, even though he said he did want to quit. She asked if I had any suggestions. I wrote:

Maybe your Rebel husband can change his way of thinking about quitting.

—Rebels hate to be trapped, constrained. So view smoking as a trap: "I'm chained by addiction; I'm helpless without my cigarettes."

—Rebels hate to be exploited: "I'm pouring money right into the pockets of the big tobacco companies."

—Rebels want to express their identity. "I'm a nonsmoker. That's the person I choose to be. That's what I want."

—Rebels value pleasure. "It will be so great to wake up without a hacking cough and bad breath, to feel more energetic, and not to huff and puff when I walk up the stairs."

—Rebels value freedom. "In places like office buildings or airports, they order me around, telling me where I have to go if I want to smoke."

—Rebels like to do things in their own way: instead of following a standard cessation program, he could come up with his own way to quit.

—NOTE: For Rebels, there's always the "I'll show you" gambit. "Honey, I think quitting smoking may just be too tough to do. Those cigarettes have really got their hooks into you. I don't think you'll ever be able to quit. Maybe you should give up trying."

She wrote back with a progress report: "The most effective strategy was an adaptation of the last point. I told him that his eighteen-year-old son thinks that an old guy like him can't quit (true), and there was a definite 'I'll show him' response."

Rebels also enjoy flouting convention and proving that they're too smart for the tricks that fool most people. One Rebel quit drinking in a very Rebel way:

> The revelation came to me that I like drinking but I don't like gaining weight, I don't like spending so much money, I don't like embarrassing myself at parties, and I don't like being hung over. Once I realized the lie the world tells us about drinking and indulgence—that skinny, beautiful people on TV drink and eat out constantly and never get sick or poor or fat—it was much easier to let go.

Rebels want to express their values through their actions, so tying a habit to an important identity can help a Rebel to change.

Choosing a Career as a Rebel

I'll say it again: Rebels can do anything they *want* to do. Recognizing this, Rebels often seek out careers that give them the flexibility to choose their work, set their own schedules, and avoid having to answer to other people. I've heard from many Rebels about how they strive to create situations where every day is different, with no set expectations from others. "I have a superflexible job schedule. I used to work in an office and really hated that. Now, as a project manager and H.R. director for a restaurant, I work from home and occasionally go into the restaurant. I make my own schedule every day, and every day is different." "I'm an IT contractor. I get bored and change jobs a lot, and fortunately, there haven't been too many periods of being out of work." "I'm a certified public accountant in a tax practice. Deadlines, and nonsensical, arbitrary rules are all I deal with! However, I do this as a self-employed person, controlling my own work life and client base."

Rebels often start their own businesses because they don't want to answer to anyone but themselves—but, of course, Rebels don't like to answer to themselves, either. I met a Rebel at a technology conference. He said, "I have to work for myself because I want to wake up every day and do only what I want."

"But," I pressed, "you've got your own business. There must be tasks you have to do, even if you don't want to."

"Well, that's a terrible problem," he admitted, deflated. "I can't make myself do that stuff until it absolutely has to be done. It's crippling my business."

One successful Rebel entrepreneur told me, "Rebels on our own aren't very effective. We don't like all the little management details, deadlines, that stuff. So I've started three companies with my wife. She's an Upholder, and she balances my Rebel side, and together we're a fantastic team."

Rebels often thrive in a situation where they're given a challenge and allowed to meet it in their own way. Perhaps that's why many Rebels gravitate toward sales—because in sales, actual results tend to be the thing that matters the most. One wife of a Rebel observed, "My husband clashes with his boss a lot, but he's also the most successful salesperson. Not 'despite' but 'because' he ignores the rules that his boss sets that would make him lose the sale."

Similarly, in creative industries, results count for the most. My sister, Elizabeth, who's a TV writer and producer, observed, "In Hollywood, Rebels can get away with flouting the rules, as long as they produce something good. Also, especially among director types, they want to do things their own way, and they don't care what other people think, and creatively, that can lead to a great outcome, even if the process is unpleasant for everybody around them."

I talked to a Rebel corporate lawyer—a job that doesn't necessarily sound like a good fit for a Rebel. "How do you do it?" I asked.

"I love it," she said. "I'm brought in during a crisis, when people are willing to take risks. If things aren't working, I break them apart, I fix whatever's wrong, then I move on. Once things are stable and rules are imposed, I find it suffocating."

At the same time, as noted earlier, Rebels may be drawn to areas of high regulation, like the police, the military, and the clergy.

SUMMARY: DEALING WITH A REBEL

They resist both outer and inner expectations

They put a high value on freedom, choice, identity, and self-expression

If someone asks or tells them to do something, they're likely to resist.

They may respond to a challenge: "I'll show you," "Watch me," "You can't make me," "You're not the boss of me"

They may choose to act out of love, a sense of mission, belief in a cause

They have trouble telling themselves what to do—even when it's something they *want* to do

They meet a challenge, in their own way, in their own time

They don't respond well to supervision, advice, or directions

They tend to be good at delegating

If they're in a long-term relationship, their partner is probably an Obliger

APPLYING THE FOUR

TENDENCIES

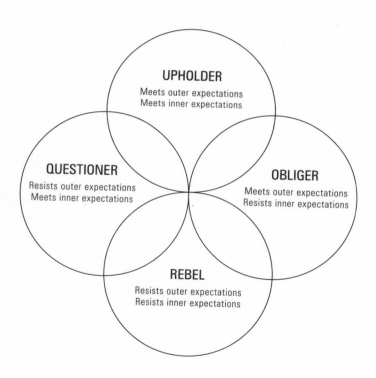

UPHOLDER
Meets outer expectations
Meets inner expectations

QUESTIONER
Resists outer expectations
Meets inner expectations

OBLIGER
Meets outer expectations
Resists inner expectations

REBEL
Resists outer expectations
Resists inner expectations

11

When the Four Tendencies Pair Up

No relationship is doomed, or assured, based on the Tendencies. Nevertheless, when people from different Tendencies pair up—as romantic partners, as parent and child, as colleagues, or any other kind of pairing—certain patterns tend to emerge.

When we first meet someone, we're often attracted to the very qualities that, over time, will drive us nuts. An Upholder might initially be intrigued by a Rebel's refusal to play by the rules, and the Rebel may be drawn to the Upholder's ability to get things done—but five years into the marriage, those qualities look much less attractive.

It's not the only thing that matters, of course, but understanding the Four Tendencies can give us a useful insight into our relationships.

Upholder-Upholder

I've talked to very few romantic pairs of Upholders, which may mean that Upholders don't pair up well or may simply reflect the fact that Upholders are fairly rare.

When I get the chance, I love working with other Upholders: I can rely on them to complete tasks without any chivvying, and they tell me frankly if I'm being too demanding.

I'm not sure I would want to be married to an Upholder, however. All that expectation-keeping might get too intense, and even if two Upholders get along well, they might make a tough environment for others. One Upholder wrote:

> My husband and I are Upholders, and as my 13-year-old daughter says, "Mom, I don't know any parents like you and Dad." I take that as a compliment. We both highly value character and discipline. I'm a health coach, and my husband is a coach and tennis director. With our clients and students, we are nothing but compassionate and caring, but "behind the scenes" we can be judgmental. We both get frustrated when others don't do what they say they're going to do.

Two Upholders are likely to get a lot done, but they'll find drawbacks, too. On a trip that my family took with another family, the Upholder husband/father of that family and I decided to take our children on a boat ride through Berlin. Along the river we could see many places to catch a tour boat, and a guide pointed to one and said, "The next boat leaves from that stand." A little later, we two Upholders stood next to this empty stand and watched as passengers boarded a boat at another stand just a few yards away.

"He told us that *this* was where the next boat would be," my friend said, as the boat departed.

"I know!" I answered. "Right?" We had to poke fun at ourselves—even though we could see that one boat stand was empty and the other was active, we'd stuck to what the "expert" had told us. I thought to myself that if Jamie had been there with us, we'd have left this stand and gone to the other one. There are advantages to having a Questioner around.

Upholder-Questioner

Upholders often pair with Questioners. That describes my marriage, and I think it's a very helpful combination, for both spouses. Upholders sometimes meet expectations too readily, so the presence of a Questioner helps them to question or reject some demands that they might otherwise thoughtlessly meet. From the Questioner perspective, Upholders are generally easy spouses, because they so readily meet expectations.

My sister pointed out that as an Upholder, I have a Questioner in two of the most influential places in my life: my husband and my literary agent, Christy Fletcher. Their questioning helps save me from doing things I don't need to do, at home and at work.

For instance, around the time of the publication of the paperback edition of *Better Than Before*, I was asked to write a magazine piece. My proposed assignment: Write a first-person story on the Four Tendencies, with a brief introduction explaining each Tendency, along with advice for each Tendency for mastering habits, in about 1,000 words. For free.

This would be a terribly demanding piece to write, and my heart sank as I read and reread the description. Then I thought of an escape. I emailed Christy to say, "Should I do this?" "No way," she wrote back instantly.

As an Upholder, being married to Questioner Jamie has helped me learn to question more myself. (In fact, perhaps Jamie wishes I'd picked up fewer of his Questioner ways; it's quite nice to have a spouse who generally does whatever's asked, without any questions.) At the same time, as an Upholder, I can get impatient with his Questioner refusal to act until all questions have been answered—not to mention the Questioner reluctance to answer questions.

Nevertheless, it's a relief for both Upholders and Questioners that their partner can readily meet their own inner expectations.

Upholder parents can get annoyed with the questions of Questioner children, because they expect their children to *just do it*. One Upholder father wrote,

> Sometimes I get frustrated parenting my Questioner child; it's hard to understand why my child just won't do what has to be done. Of course all little kids can be frustrating. But to my mind, things like putting on shoes, getting spelling done, having a shower, are just things that have to be done, so the child should just get on with it. But for a Questioner child, everything is a negotiation.

Upholder-Obliger

Like all the Tendencies, Upholders pair well with Obligers. Obligers and Upholders both share a desire to meet outer expectations (unlike Questioners and Rebels) and so will cooperate and respect that desire in each other.

Upholders are gratified by the Obligers' (mostly) reliable meeting of outer expectations, but they can become frustrated by Obligers' inability to meet their own inner expectations.

Also, they may be very unsympathetic to Obligers who feel pressured by expectations. For instance, an Obliger might tell an Upholder boss, "I'm exhausted, because I've stayed up until 3:00 a.m. for the past five nights to get the report ready for you." Instead of answering with the appreciation that the Obliger expects, the Upholder might well say, "You need to learn to manage your workflow so you don't have to work these intense hours. To be at the top of your game, you need sleep."

For their part, Obligers appreciate the Upholders' meeting of outer expectations. However, they can get overwhelmed by what Upholders expect, and they may feel judged by Upholders, who may have little understanding of why Obligers might struggle to meet inner expectations.

Obligers sometimes find Upholders cold or selfish, because Upholders may choose to meet an inner expectation even when it conflicts with an outer expectation. One Obliger (who sounds primed for a major spell of Obliger-rebellion) wrote:

> During our nine-year marriage, my Upholder husband has completed medical school, residency, and is now working. He was a very intense student, and I was excited when his exams were done. I thought I'd finally have my whole husband. To my disappointment, I've realized that he will always have a major goal or project that he's working on. And because I'm an Obliger, I feel like I internalize his goals,

which means that I've often "picked up the slack" for him in areas that traditionally are a man's domain so he could focus on school, etc.

But now I don't feel his goals benefit the whole family, and I get annoyed that he's seeking "extra" things and has fixed deadlines for things that I don't find important. We have three small kids that he helps a ton with, true. But I still feel like he's rushing through helping with them to get to his own goals. He also gets up super-early (5:00 a.m.) to accomplish things—and he often wakes me up. After being up with babies or kids multiple times each night, and after many years of sleep deprivation, it really annoys me to get woken up for his goals.

He acts like he has so much to do, but in my mind he doesn't, because these things aren't outer expectations. At a time when I'm barely hanging on by a thread, I want him to focus on basics and not take on extra goals that inevitably become my goals, too. If I act disinterested in his goals, then I might as well not be around, because that's all that seems important to him.

I can appreciate both perspectives there. I have to say, as an Upholder, this Obliger's lament gave me a whole new insight into why Obligers get impatient with Upholders.

Obligers may get frustrated when Upholders refuse to provide accountability.

Upholders may feel uncomfortable when Obligers say, "I'm doing this because you told me to do it" or "I'm doing this for you." Upholders want people to do things for their own reasons—which is a big demand.

Understanding the Tendencies can help reduce conflict. One Upholder wrote, "Learning that my partner is an

Obliger improved our relationship, because now I understand that if he doesn't follow through on something, it isn't because he's careless or undisciplined. He just needs outer accountability."

Upholder-Rebel

In general, Upholders and Rebels don't pair up easily. They see the world in very different ways and thrive in very different environments. Breaking the rules makes the Upholder uneasy, while the Rebel gets a kick out of it. Over time, this can lead to a lot of problems. As one reader wrote: "I'm an Upholder married to a Rebel. He has great difficulty working under bosses, hates our church, is unhappy most of the time that he has to work. He only does jobs around the home that he selects and wants to do. I go to a counselor myself, but he won't go. I do love him. He was my white knight through a very difficult cancer treatment (no sign of the Rebel then!)."

Also, Upholders tend to love schedules, plans, and assignments, and dislike changes of plans or failure to complete them, while Rebels resist binding commitments. The more the Upholder tries to put something on the calendar or to-do list, the more the Rebel wants to ignore it.

The Upholder-Rebel matchup can be tough when it involves a parent and a child, no matter who's the Upholder and who's the Rebel.

A Rebel friend has a young Upholder son. I asked, "Say your son's school had a rule like 'Children have to wear button-down shirts on Friday.' What would you do?"

She considered for a moment. "If it were important to him, I'd buy him the shirt," she said. (She's a Rebel who puts great emphasis on being a loving, understanding parent.) "But I would never *make* him wear the shirt."

As always, whether an Upholder and a Rebel can pair up successfully will depend on their other personality traits. For instance, in marriage, an Upholder might pair well with a Rebel who puts a high value on the identity of being a loving, helpful partner.

And an Upholder and a Rebel can get along well in a relationship where they don't have many expectations for each other. One Rebel wrote, "My Upholder roommate was absolutely horrified that I get up at a different time every day. I was horrified by the fact that she's so regimented that she recognizes the other people in her subway car!" While they're astonished by each other's behavior, their own lives aren't affected by it, so it doesn't hurt their friendship.

The fact is, no combination of Tendencies is doomed; given the right combination of personalities and circumstances, any pair can work. As one Upholder explained:

> My partner's Rebel Tendency balances me and helps me tone down my Upholder side. I love being an Upholder, but there have been times when it was my downfall—particularly when I was struggling with realizing I was gay. Coming out felt like letting myself and my family's expectations down simultaneously, which for an Upholder was almost too much to bear.
>
> By contrast, my partner never struggled with coming out when she was younger, because she was more than happy to go against the grain. As a result, her Rebel Tendency helped protect her emotionally during what for most people is an extremely trying period of self-discovery. Her confidence in who she is is one of the things I've always admired about her.

Her spontaneity can be frustrating, but it also forces me to lighten up and realize when I'm "upholding for the sake of upholding." For example, I struggle with canceling plans, but if I'm not feeling well or have had a stressful week, she takes pleasure in watching me finally bend and cancel, which counterbalances the feeling that I've not met expectations I placed on myself. And despite her Rebel tendency, she does want to make me happy and will therefore acquiesce to my lists, calendars, and the endless planning that I inject into our daily lives (though she does bring a fair dose of humor to it).

Another Rebel explained why she thinks the Upholder-Rebel pairing can be a good match: "I admire my Upholder husband's extreme dedication and tireless pursuit of his goals. He values my independence and nonconformist thinking. We both belong to the two 'extreme' tendencies, and neither of us really understands Obligers or Questioners. To us, they seem inconsistent and mushy."

Upholders and Rebels can learn a lot from each other. I'd written that my Upholder motto is "Discipline brings freedom," and a thoughtful Rebel replied, "As a motto for us Rebels, I propose flipping your Upholder motto, Gretchen, on its head. Upholders and Rebels could, after all, be described as antithetical. So while you live by the motto, 'Discipline brings freedom,' I live by the motto: 'Freedom is my discipline.'"

Questioner-Questioner

For some people, the pairing of two Questioners works well, because both partners understand and appreciate the importance of getting answers to questions. One Questioner explained:

> My husband and I are both Questioners, in different ways. He'll spend hours researching a purchase like a tent for camping, and I would never do this (I make quick decisions regarding purchases), but even though I wouldn't do it, I find satisfaction in knowing that he did the research.
>
> I've observed how different we are from some couples, because we don't feel threatened or criticized when we question each other. We understand the need to look at a decision from multiple angles—we find it helpful instead of hurtful. It's refreshing that he doesn't feel criticized when I question decisions, purchases, plans. He gets it, he even appreciates it.

On the other hand, two Questioners can sometimes find it hard to make decisions. A Questioner friend observed, "Because we're both Questioners, we can get stuck."

"Like what?"

"When we were renovating our house, we needed to replace our dishwasher, and every time we'd go to replace it, next thing you know, we're standing out in the yard deciding whether to add a second floor. Every question seemed to lead to more questions."

"So how did you two finally decide?"

"For a good two years, we lived with a nonfunctioning dishwasher, because we just couldn't decide what to do. Finally I decided that *any* dishwasher is better than *no* dishwasher. I said, 'We're having houseguests next month, and we have to get the new dishwasher installed by that date.' We both respond well to deadlines."

The pairing of Questioner parent and Questioner child often works well. The parent sympathizes with the child's resistance to doing anything arbitrary or unjustified, and may be willing to give reasons for parenting judgments. The Questioner child respects the Questioner parent's sound decision making.

However, the Questioner's dislike of being questioned can cause frustration. The Questioner parent says, "We'll eat whatever I cook for dinner," or the Questioner child says, "I'm dealing with my science project, I don't want to talk about it." Explanations exist—these are Questioners, after all—but Questioners often don't want to be questioned.

Questioner-Obliger

Obligers team up well with Questioners, but there are potential points of conflict. One Obliger gave a small but telling example: "I use crosswalks and follow the walk signals, while my Questioner husband doesn't find it important to use crosswalks or signals, so he jaywalks."

Obligers can get exasperated by Questioners' constant demand for reasons, information, and justifications. One Obliger recalled:

> I worked for a Questioner boss who could never get enough information to make a decision until the very last minute. As an Obliger who did financial modeling and forecasting for her, I spent countless hours creating new models with slightly different assumptions that all ended up with nearly the same answer as the original model.

Obligers do well to remember that Questioners are much more cooperative when they understand why they're being asked to do something. One Obliger wrote, "Now I know that when I ask my Questioner husband to do something, I need to explain why it's important. I'm used to thinking that if it needs to get done, then he should just do it, but he needs a reason to do it. We've had hours-long 'discussions' that we could've avoided if I'd just known to give him the whys up front."

An Obliger parent can get very impatient with a Questioner child, whose questions can seem tiresome or cheeky. An Obliger told me:

> As an Obliger, my view is that if your parent, teacher, or coach tells you to do something, you do it—no questions asked. But my Questioner daughter refuses to do anything until she understands why she's being asked to do it. I know that she doesn't mean to sound smart-alecky or uncooperative, but I worry that other adults in her life won't be so patient.

When Questioners see Obligers fail to meet an inner expectation, they can sometimes be dismissive or harsh; because they don't have trouble meeting inner expectations, they have little sympathy for Obligers' struggle. Similarly, when Obligers complain about something they "have" to do, Questioners don't have much sympathy, because they think, "If you don't want to do it, don't do it" or "Why did you say you'd do it, if you don't want to?"

Questioner-Rebel

Questioners and Rebels have an affinity. Both Tendencies feel justified—to a greater or lesser degree—in setting the rules for themselves and rejecting outer expectations. One Rebel wrote, "I get along well with Questioners. They're like 'I don't care what people say we're supposed to do, that doesn't make sense for me, I won't do it. What about you?' and I'm like 'Oh, I don't feel like doing it, either.'"

To Upholders and Obligers, this attitude can sometimes look like a self-involved disregard for expectations intended to apply to everyone. But Questioners and Rebels are amazed that anyone would behave otherwise.

However, Questioners can get impatient with the Rebels' automatic contrarian position and refusal to do what's fair or efficient or reasonable; Rebels are unmoved by the Questioners' insistence on information and justifications. I heard from a reader:

> I'm a Questioner, and now there's a Rebel in my office. He does his own thing when the group has already decided on another course of action. He wastes time on things that don't add value. I love my job, because my job is to ask why things are the way they are and to come up with answers based on data and research. But I come home frustrated because this person ignores new data and research and focuses on what he feels he should be doing instead. I'm frustrated because he misses deadlines, and my own questions aren't answered.

One Questioner partnered with a Rebel set out the pros and cons of this matchup:

> We really understand each other when we make off-the-wall choices that go against the mainstream, because I've researched and feel good about it, and it makes him oddly happy to do something unexpected. On the other hand,

decisions like car choices can hang us up. I'll drown in research, and he's terrified at the prospect of being "bound" to the same car. We both frequently agree outer expectations mean nothing to us.

Obliger-Obliger

Depending on the circumstances, a relationship between two Obligers can be very harmonious—two of the happiest married couples I know are Obliger-Obliger—but they can also struggle to get into action. An Obliger explained, "We want to eat healthfully, but when one of us says 'Want to get pizza?' the other one says 'Heck, yes!' We have a hard time being motivated to do healthy activities together, such as exercise. It's easy to make grand plans for everything we could do, and then it doesn't happen."

The key for Obliger-Obliger pairs is to set up systems of outer accountability—which may often mean accountability outside the pair. A married couple who wants to stick to a budget might struggle to hold each other accountable, but regular meetings with a financial adviser or coach might give them accountability.

An Obliger parent with an Obliger child can work well. Parents feel accountable for their children, and children feel accountable to their parents, so together they can get a lot accomplished. One Obliger wrote:

> I needed accountability to get me out of bed in the morning. My mom wanted to get up early, too, so I proposed that we be Bible buddies. I call her at 7:00 a.m., and we have a quick catch-up, then we read a passage and discuss it, then we pray

for each other. It's the perfect solution, because it gets us out of bed and also instills a new habit of reading the Bible daily, which I've always wanted to do. Plus it makes us both really happy to share this time together.

Obliger-Rebel

This very striking pattern of pairing is discussed in chapter 10, in the section "Dealing with a Rebel Spouse—and the Pattern of the Rebel/Obliger Couple."

Some Obliger-Rebel pairs do experience frustration. For instance, many Obliger adult children have told me that it's tough to have a Rebel parent.

A friend said, "My mother adores her grandchildren, but if I ask her to babysit, she wants us to bring the kids to her house, at the time she chooses. Everything has to be on her terms. And she misses out because of it. My husband and I often don't include her because we think, 'Well, we want to get there on time, or do things a certain way, and she won't go along with it.'"

Another Obliger wrote to me, "I once told my father that something started at 6:00, when it started at 7:00, because he's chronically late. He told me that I'd been manipulative. Fair enough."

Manipulative—or realistic? It's a fine line.

Rebel-Rebel

Rebels often don't tend to pair up well with other Rebels. An Obliger observed, "My husband and daughter are both

Rebels, and ironically they both hate the Rebel streaks in each other. They judge each other most harshly for doing exactly what the other does—they call each other lazy, point out each other's faults, and clash all the time."

A reader wrote to me: "I know one Rebel-Rebel pairing, and it works for two reasons: (1) The husband makes a lot of money at his own business, which he loves obsessively, and his wife stays home and does whatever she feels like after getting the kids off to school. (2) They both have strong identities that make them want to be good parents and family members."

I was intrigued by this rare spotting of a Rebel-Rebel pair, so I wrote to ask, "How do they decide what to do? Say, when and where to go on a vacation?" Rebels generally resist being told to do a certain thing at a certain time, even if they want to do it.

My source wrote back:

> I love hearing their vacation planning stories. The wife picks exactly what she wants, and then the husband decides whether he wants to go as well. So far, he's rarely wanted to be left behind, but she puts no obligations on him to go. If he'd asked her to book that vacation, she would've resisted. They plan most events this way: one person cares very much, and the other person shows up, or doesn't. When it comes to kid obligations, they take turns as much as possible, because each of them finds it painful to do what they're "supposed" to do. I don't think their relationship would work if they couldn't afford to outsource so much.

One Rebel-Rebel pair described their relationship:

> I'm the type I would call "the libertarian rebel" [REBEL/ Obliger]. I need autonomy, space, freedom, flexibility, to

move often, to change perspective, not to feel bound too strictly. I want to change plans the very moment a plan starts forming in my head. My husband is different, but still a Rebel. I'd call him "the identitarian rebel" [REBEL/Questioner]. He wants to be original, do things his own way, be true to himself, express himself in what he does and how he does it.

As for our life together, to be honest, there's not much of that. I work in a different town, so we're a living-apart-together couple. We have two flats. Every time we spend some days together, I start feeling restless. Neither of us sees the point of devoting much thought, time, energy, or money into keeping the flats in order, so we devote very little time to these chores.

These two Rebels make a successful couple because they've set up their lives to work for them instead of trying to follow a conventional model.

I've talked to many people who've told me, "I'm a Rebel with a Rebel child, and I don't know how non-Rebels figure out how to handle a Rebel kid." Though one Rebel mother told me, "I used to feel guilty about the fact that I wasn't checking up on my daughter, reminding her to do her homework, or anything like that. Now that I realize that she's a Rebel just like me, I know that it's better not to do those things."

Some of these Tendency pairs tend to work together more harmoniously than others, and a lot depends on the situation. But when conflicts arise within a pair, whether at home or at work, there's one rule that can eliminate a lot of conflict: Whenever possible, we should allow others to do things in the way that works for them.

This sounds obvious, but in many cases, our Tendency—

as well as human nature—makes us want to dictate to other people, when we're better off letting them do things their own way.

For instance, as an Upholder, I always want to follow the rules and to get tasks done immediately; as a Questioner, Jamie always wants to do what seems most efficient. The solution? I handle my tasks in my way, he handles his tasks in his way, and neither of us interferes in the other's business.

We may think we know the "best" way, or the way others "should" work, but whether at home or at work, as long as the tasks are getting done, we should let other people suit themselves. We get along best with others when we recognize and respect that they might approach the world in a different way.

12

Speaking Effectively to Each Tendency

W hether we're at work, at home, or out in the world, we're all constantly trying to persuade or influence people to do what we want them to do (even if what we want them to do is to leave us alone). When we consider our own Tendency, we can create circumstances and messages that will work best for us, and when we consider other people's Tendencies, we can create circumstances and messages that will work best for them.

It's all too easy to assume that what persuades us will persuade others—which isn't true. One of my Secrets of Adulthood is that we're *more* like other people than we suppose and *less* like other people than we suppose. And it's very hard to keep that in mind.

In a nutshell, to influence someone to follow a certain course, it's helpful to remember:

- Upholders want to know what should be done
- Questioners want justifications

- Obligers need accountability

- Rebels want freedom to do something their own way

Similarly, we're more likely to be persuasive when we invoke the values that have special appeal for a particular Tendency:

- Upholders value self-command and performance

- Questioners value justification and purpose

- Obligers value teamwork and duty

- Rebels value freedom and self-identity

Because the Tendencies see the world in such different ways, there are no magic, one-size-fits-all solutions for how to influence ourselves or other people. I exercise regularly because it's on my to-do list; a Questioner rattles off the health benefits; an Obliger takes a weekly bike ride because he's found an exercise partner; and a Rebel runs when it suits her, whenever she feels like being outside.

My Questioner father told me how he quit smoking: "Your mother and I were still struggling with money, and I'd calculate how much money I'd save by not buying cigarettes—and then if I invested that money, how much I'd make." He crunched the numbers and focused on the benefits of quitting. By contrast, an Obliger friend quit smoking by thinking about his obligation to his baby son: "Now that I have a child, I can't take stupid health risks. And I want to be a good role model." A Rebel tells herself, "I refuse to be a slave to nicotine addiction."

Understanding the Four Tendencies helps us to identify how we might help others, by playing the role they need.

For instance, for people with diabetes, it's important to take medication consistently, eat right, exercise, and see the doctor. My sister Elizabeth has type 1 diabetes, and she told me, "My diabetes doctor told me that some people stop going to him because they say he's 'too nice.'"

"'Too nice,' meaning what?" I asked.

"Not tough enough with them, if they don't do all the things they're supposed to do."

"I bet those are Obligers who need more accountability!" I said. "For you, having regular appointments with your doctor is enough to hold you accountable, but some Obligers need more consequences. They'll switch doctors to get more accountability." With the Four Tendencies in mind, her doctor could adapt his relationships with patients to give them the type of accountability they need to succeed.

Some people in health care have already started using the Four Tendencies.

I'm a textbook Upholder. I work as a clinical dietitian at the Mayo Clinic, in the outpatient (clinic) setting. I've been confused by why some patients struggle to make changes to their eating habits. Most know that their disease management and health would improve if they changed their eating habits, yet many don't make changes. Understanding the Four Tendencies has revolutionized my thinking and has drastically improved the quality of care I am able to provide to my patients.

Similarly, a physiologist reported:

I work in cardiac rehabilitation, and a big part of my job is encouraging healthy behavior change. I can now clearly put people into different Tendencies.

Upholder: "This is something that should be done. I've got it."

Questioner: "Why should I be doing this? Give me the evidence, I want reasons."

Obliger: "Let me show you how well I can do this."

Rebel: "Don't tell me what to eat or how to exercise."

With more frustration, one reader wrote: "I like my therapist, but I've told her about needing external accountability, and she just doesn't seem to buy it. She's convinced I need to 'motivate myself' and 'do things for myself.' Of course, that's not working, just as it never has in my entire life. I just want to do whatever will work."

I've heard this so many times, and I have to say, I don't understand why people seem to view it as a problem—or, worse, as *shameful*—to need outer accountability to follow through. My own feeling is—whatever works for you, fine! Just figure it out.

People often want to change a habit—one of their own or someone else's. And one of the worst, most common mistakes when we're trying to help someone change a habit? Invoking the dreaded "You should be able to . . ."

- "If good health is important to you, you should be able to exercise on your own."

- "If you take this job seriously, you should be able to stick to this schedule I've drawn up."

- "If you want to make a sale, you should be able to bend the rules."

- "If you respect me, you should be able to do what I tell you to do, with no talking back."

- "If you respect yourself, you should be able to make time for your writing."

But it doesn't matter what we think a person (or ourselves) "should be able to" do—what matters is *only what works for each individual*. To help people change their habits or behavior, we should help get them what they need to succeed, whether that's more clarity, more information, more outer accountability, or more choices.

A reader wrote, "I'm an Obliger and my husband is a Questioner. Only when I told him about your framework did he understand why I want him to ask me if I've eaten healthy that day (for accountability). Before that, he thought it was a really weird request, because if I wanted to eat healthy, why didn't I just make up my mind to do so?"

When we understand the Four Tendencies, we can set up situations to work better for everyone. Say a manager runs a mixed-Tendency team. At the meeting where he announces that the company is adopting a new processing system, he could give the presentation, then say, "If you feel that you've heard enough about the new system and why we're switching, feel free to get back to your desk. If you'd like to learn more, please stay, and I'll answer all your questions." This way, he saves the time of anyone who doesn't need further explanation (mainly Obligers and Upholders), and gives others (probably mostly Questioners) the information they need to embrace the change. Rebels will go whenever they feel like going.

To reach every student in class, a professor could explain

the purpose of all class requirements: "Over the years, students have found that writing article summaries helps them to assimilate information, plus the summaries are invaluable when you're studying for exams." Over the semester, the professor could require monthly check-in emails so that students update her on their writing progress. She might offer three possible assignments from which to choose instead of just one. By taking the Four Tendencies into account, she helps her students succeed.

Some mistakes are common. When trying to persuade someone, Upholders and Questioners often emphasize the importance of getting clarity on inner expectations. "You need to decide what you want," "You need to get clear on your intentions," "Figure out your priorities, what's right for you"—great advice, *for other Upholders or Questioners.* Obligers often make arguments like "This will inconvenience someone else," "You have to do this, it's part of your job," "It's not right to expect someone else to do that"—great arguments, *for other Obligers.*

A teacher wrote:

> I think all strong teachers use the Tendencies, even if they don't realize it. Here's an example: My students are four and five and still nap at school. Most still need naps but don't want to settle down. Here's how I handle it:
>
> Upholders: "We've had a busy day. You were running a lot, and we have a game we're going to play when we wake up. I want you to be rested for that."
>
> Questioners: "Why do you think I ask you to take a nap each day? Why are naps important?" They answer with ideas. I say, "Right! So do you agree that you should try to rest?" (They say yes, because it makes sense to them.)

Obligers: "I'd be so proud if you took a good nap like yesterday. I know you can, and your body will feel so good when you wake up."

Rebels: "You don't have to nap, but will you please stay quiet on your cot for a few minutes? If you're not tired after that, you can read a book." (They like knowing that sleeping is their decision and invariably end up napping.)

Reflecting on the Four Tendencies often makes it clear why we're not getting along with someone else. We often madden one another with our Tendencies. For instance, an Upholder might keep admonishing a team, "If you just make up your mind to do it, you'll do it!"; a Questioner might keep emailing productivity studies to an Obliger coworker; an Obliger might sign up a Rebel for a weekly exercise class; a Rebel might urge an Upholder to stop being so uptight. This miscommunication, while well intentioned, leads to frustration.

In some situations, Four Tendencies–based miscommunication can become downright dangerous. If a police officer says, "Step out of the car," the Questioner or Rebel may argue: "Why should I?" "What gives you the right to ask me to do that?" "I wasn't doing anything, this is an arbitrary stop." "You can't order me around." The more the officer gives orders, the more he or she will arouse a spirit of resistance. From there, a situation may escalate.

I love spotting signage that succeeds or fails to engage the Four Tendencies. We can invite cooperation from all the Tendencies or trigger resistance, depending on how we frame a message.

To craft a sign that works well for all Four Tendencies, we should provide information, consequences, and choice. This is the sequence that works for Rebels, of course, plus

Questioners cooperate better when they have information and justification, and Obligers, when they know consequences. Upholders tend to follow a rule.

I couldn't resist taking a photo when I visited a company and saw this overwrought sign posted in a stall in the women's bathroom. It does *not* do a good job of reaching all Four Tendencies.

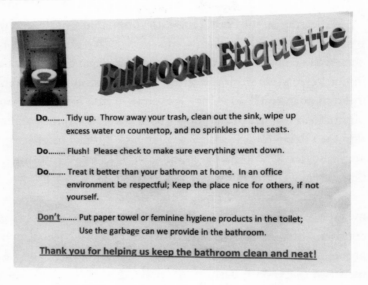

Bathroom Etiquette

Do........ Tidy up. Throw away your trash, clean out the sink, wipe up excess water on countertop, and no sprinkles on the seats.

Do........ Flush! Please check to make sure everything went down.

Do........ Treat it better than your bathroom at home. In an office environment be respectful; Keep the place nice for others, if not yourself.

<u>Don't</u>........ Put paper towel or feminine hygiene products in the toilet; Use the garbage can we provide in the bathroom.

<u>**Thank you for helping us keep the bathroom clean and neat!**</u>

This sign was written by an Obliger, for Obligers—note the Obliger-aimed "Keep the place nice for others, if not for yourself." To convince a Rebel, the *opposite* would be more effective: "Keep the place nice for yourself, if not for others." Plus all those pushy "dos" and "don'ts" might push a Rebel—or, possibly, a Questioner or even an Upholder like me—to resist.

It's surprisingly easy for a sign to trigger resistance. A Rebel wrote, "When I see those 'Thank you for not smoking' or whatever, it makes me want to smoke, even though I don't smoke! I hate the implication that because they've ordered me to do it, I'll do it."

On the other hand, when I took my seat in the writing room of my beloved New York Society Library, I noticed a clever posting that needed very few words to appeal to all Four Tendencies:

It appeals to Upholders: Here are the rules, follow them. It appeals to Questioners: The reason for the rule "No food or drink" is that food and drink attract bugs, and bugs damage books. It appeals to Obligers: The librarians know that people have been breaking the rules, because we have ants, so stop! And it appeals to Rebels: The people using the writing room are bookish types who value the library, so they'd choose to act in a way that protects the collection and respects the request of librarians—plus, who wants to work someplace that's crawling with ants?

The sign from a bathroom in the Willard Hotel in Washington, D.C., does a good job of appealing to Upholders, Questioners, Obligers, and Rebels. Note the final line—in a large font—aimed directly at Rebels.

Our efforts continue to
conserve & reduce.

Reusing towels
eliminates the disposal of thousands of gallons of detergent and water each year.

If you intend to reuse your towels, please hang them up.

If not, please leave them in the bathtub.

We appreciate your support of the program, and as always the choice is yours.

The Ritz-Carlton hotel on Amelia Island, Florida, clearly had trouble with guests who left the sliding doors open. I can imagine some people thinking, "What do I care if there's heavy condensation? That's a long-term problem for the hotel. But no air-conditioning and flying insects? That's a problem right now for *me*."

This sign does a good job of connecting with all Four Tendencies: information, consequences, choice. Plus an appeal to identity never hurts.

For an important message to be effective, it needs to resonate with every Tendency. When Hurricane Sandy was due to hit New York City, Mayor Michael Bloomberg ordered people in vulnerable neighborhoods to evacuate, but many refused to go—something that I, as an Upholder, found astonishing.

How might a mayor word an evacuation notice in order to persuade people of all Four Tendencies?

Upholders would evacuate if the expectation is established, so the notice should state clearly that people are expected to leave. Upholders wouldn't take much convincing.

Questioners would evacuate if they were convinced that this action made sense, so the notice should give ample justification for when, where, and with what strength the hurricane would hit, what the risks were, why actual evacuation was necessary, why each particular neighborhood was at risk, why a well-built or elevated home was nevertheless at risk. The notice should also explain what experts—meteorologists, engineers, architects—had been consulted. Be wary of comparing this storm to a previous storm, because if a person didn't have trouble during that storm, he or she might conclude that this storm will be no more dangerous.

Obligers would evacuate if there's external accountability, so the notice should emphasize that failure to evacuate would put family members as well as first responders at risk, that city workers would know whether residents have evacuated, that penalties would be imposed on those refusing to leave. It should remind people of their obligation to keep family members and neighbors safe, and to act as role models of good citizenship. It should emphasize that the best way to care for others (including pets) was to find a way to evacuate.

Rebels hate to be told what to do, but they'd be more willing to evacuate if staying put would limit their freedom and comfort. The notice should emphasize that people who stayed behind would be trapped in place, perhaps for days, and that conditions in their homes would be dangerous at worst, unpleasant at best—with a likely loss of electricity, running water, elevators, and public transportation. And no Chinese takeout.

Also: The mayor should also inform people that their names will be noted; no matter what our Tendency, we may behave differently if we're acting anonymously.

Because of my quest to discover Four Tendencies signage, I always glance into the office kitchen when I visit a company; the signs on various fridges and sinks make a wonderful study in how we can be more—or less—persuasive. On the Better app, I sparked a spirited Tendencies debate with the question, "Dirty dishes in the office kitchen sink: what's the best signage?"

One Obliger proposed this sign:

Thank you for taking care of your own dishes. Place them in the dishwasher. If the dishwasher is full, empty it and re-load it. If the dishwasher is running, put rinsed dishes in the sink and come back later to take care of them. Your mother isn't here to clean up after you.

Wow, I thought, there are *so many reasons* why that sign won't work.

Some good ideas didn't involve signs at all. For instance, give everyone a personalized mug; the impulse to take care of "my mug" is stronger—plus it's not possible to shirk anonymously.

But for signage, our group conclusion was that the winning formula is indeed information-consequences-choice, or perhaps no sign at all—and best of all, *humor*. A humorous sign can make a point in a way that's informative, memorable, and doesn't ignite the spirit of resistance; the right cartoon from *Dilbert* or *The New Yorker* can work better than a paragraph of directions. I remember a sign I saw at a swimming pool: "We don't swim in your toilet. Please don't pee in our pool." For the office kitchen, a Rebel suggested this sign: "If the kitchen stays clean, we'll take down the signs telling people to keep the kitchen clean."

In just about all situations, framing expectations to suit the Four Tendencies can bring more cooperation and completion, with less friction. In most cases, when we try to influence others, we use the strategies that would work on *us*. The Four Tendencies can help us, instead, to give other people what *they* need—not what *we* would need. And then we can work together more harmoniously.

13

Whatever Our Tendency, We Can Learn to Harness Its Strengths

Just as coffee can grow...under 7,000 [feet] and cedar over 7,000, I think that every human being requires a certain type of soil, temperature, and altitude, very narrowly defined for some, almost universal for others—in order to feel free and happy, that is to say, free to develop his nature to the utmost of which it is capable. I believe that one can feel completely free both in a Trappist monastery or at the court in Berlin; but I think it would have to be an unusual and an unusually gracious personality that would feel free in both places.

—Isak Dinesen, letter, August 19, 1923

Our Tendencies shape our experiences and our perspective. We respond to circumstances and language in different ways, and we flourish in different environments.

But whatever our Tendency, with greater experience and wisdom, we can learn to harness its strengths and counterbalance its negative aspects.

One afternoon, after I gave a talk about the Four Tendencies, a man asked me, "Which Tendency makes people the happiest?" I was startled to realize that this very obvious question had never crossed my mind. "Also," he continued, with an equally obvious follow-up question, "which Tendency is the most successful?"

I realized that the answer is—as it is so often—"It depends." It depends on how a particular person deals with the upside and downside of a Tendency. The happiest and most successful people are those who have figured out ways to exploit their Tendency to their benefit and, just as important, found ways to counterbalance its limitations. For all of us, it's possible to take the steps to create the life we want—but we must do that in the way that's right *for us.*

I'm haunted by a single line spoken by the novelist and Rebel John Gardner: "Every time you break the law you pay, and every time you obey the law you pay." Upholders, Questioners, Obligers, and Rebels, we all must grapple with the consequences of our Tendency—with its strengths and its weaknesses, its foibles and its frustrations.

When we understand our Tendency, we're better able to grasp how, and when, and why to pay—and how to build the life we want.

APPENDIX

ACKNOWLEDGMENTS

What a joy it was to write *The Four Tendencies*! I have so many people to thank for their help and insights in understanding the Four Tendencies.

First, thanks to my family—they've all listened to me talk about the Four Tendencies practically every day for several years.

Thanks to my brilliant agent, Christy Fletcher, and to Sylvie Greenberg, Grainne Fox, Sarah Fuentes, and Mink Choi of Fletcher & Co.

Thanks to my terrific editor, Mary Reynics, and to the extraordinary team of Diana Baroni, Sarah Breivogel, Julie Cepler, Aaron Wehner, and everyone who worked with me on *The Four Tendencies*.

And thanks as well to Lisa Highton of Two Roads.

Beth Rashbaum labored mightily to help me convey my ideas clearly.

Mike Courtney and Quyen Nguyen at Aperio Insights did an extraordinary job of building and supervising the Four Tendencies Quiz.

Thanks to the great people at Worthy Marketing—Jayme Johnson, Jody Matchett, David Struve, and everyone there.

Crystal Ellefsen helps me every day to get my words out into the world.

Mighty Networks built, maintains, and advises on the Better app. A huge thanks to Gina Bianchini, Audra Lindsay, Brian Vu, Rachel Masters, and everyone at Mighty Networks.

In podcast land, I want to thank the great people of Panoply: our terrific producer, Kristen Meinzer, former producer Henry Molofsky, as well as Andy Bowers and Laura Mayer. And also thanks to my cohost, my sister the sage, Elizabeth Craft.

FLASH EVALUATION FOR GRETCHEN RUBIN'S FOUR TENDENCIES

Many readers have requested a quick, informal method to figure out someone's Tendency.

I've heard from managers who need to make hiring decisions, teachers who want to understand their students, health professionals who want to tailor their approach to suit individual patients, people going on first dates who want to assess a potential partner—and people who just want to use the Four Tendencies as a cocktail-party ice-breaker.

A few questions can provide a strong sense of a person's Tendency. It's important not to listen for a specific "answer," but to pay attention to people's reasoning, the kind of language they use. People's answers are less important than the way they think about the question.

Because the Tendencies overlap with each other, two Tendencies might answer a particular question in the same way.

Note that Questioner and Obliger are the biggest Tendencies, so you're more likely to be dealing with a Questioner or an Obliger.

Of course, depending on the situation, people may not be truthful, for fear that an honest answer would reflect poorly on them.

"How do you feel about New Year's resolutions?"

In general, Upholders enjoy New Year's resolutions and will also make resolutions at other times.

Questioners will make and keep resolutions, but they often object that January 1 is an arbitrary date or that it's inefficient to wait to start a resolution.

Obligers often say that they no longer make New Year's resolutions because they've failed so often in the past. Or if they do make them, they often don't keep them.

Generally, Rebels won't bind themselves with resolutions. Occasionally, Rebels find it fun to do so, and they emphasize that they wanted to do it, they enjoyed it, they liked the challenge.

"Imagine that you see a sign on the wall here that says 'No cell phones,' and I pulled out my cell phone and started using it. How would you feel about that?"

Upholders will say they'd feel very uncomfortable.

Questioners will analyze the possible justifications for the rule and decide whether it is warranted. If they think the rule is senseless, they won't be bothered by seeing someone break it.

Obligers will say that they'd feel uncomfortable, which they might explain by saying that cell phone use in public places can inconvenience or annoy others, or you might get reprimanded for using a phone.

Rebels will say that they don't care. They might even get a kick out of the rule-breaking.

"Would you ever sign up to take a free course for fun? And if you did, let's say someone close to you says, 'It's kind of inconvenient for me for you to take that class.' How might you react?"

Most people will probably say something like "Well, it would depend on why it's inconvenient, how serious the inconvenience is, how important it is to me to take the course, etc." Assure them that the course would mean a very minor inconvenience for the other person.

Upholders will tend to say they'd go. They want to go; they signed up for it; they're sorry that someone else is slightly inconvenienced, but they can live with that. They will emphasize the value of sticking to plans, following through on their expectations for themselves.

Questioners, ditto. But Questioners might also focus on the reasons and justifications for their decision to take the course in the first place.

Obligers will waver when they think that someone else might be inconvenienced. That outer expectation will be painful.

Rebels will say that they wouldn't go if they didn't feel like it. They might observe that they'd never sign up for a course—how could they know what they'd feel like doing that day? If they did sign up, they wouldn't go if they didn't feel like it.

"Looking back, can you remember a time when you succeeded in changing an important habit?"

An answer such as "For years, I walked every morning with a neighbor—but she moved away, and I don't do it anymore" suggests Obligers, while "I read a lot of the new research about the value of strength-training, and after interviewing a few trainers, I now strength-train regularly" suggests Questioners, and "I run when I feel like it" suggests Rebels. Upholders will have many examples.

"Do you find it easy to complete your own to-do list? What about someone else's to-do list?"

Upholders complete their own to-do lists as easily as they complete to-do lists that others gave them.

Questioners more easily complete a to-do list they wrote themselves.

Obligers more easily complete a to-do list that someone else gave them.

Rebels usually ignore a to-do list, or they may put a Rebel spin on it, such as "I keep a running to-do list, and when I feel like tackling some chore, I'll do it, but only when I'm in the mood."

Even quicker questions to ask:

"Do people ever call you rigid?"

"Yes" suggests Upholders.

"Have people ever told you that you ask too many questions?"

"Yes" suggests Questioners.

"Do you agree: Promises we make to others shouldn't be broken, but promises we make to ourselves can be broken?"

"Yes" suggests Obligers.

"Do you think that something's more fun if it's against the rules?"

"Yes" suggests Rebels.

For each Tendency, one question matters most:

- Upholders ask: "Should I do this?"

- Questioners ask: "Does this make sense?"

- Obligers ask: "Does this matter to anyone else?"

- Rebels ask: "Is this the person I want to be?"

FURTHER RESOURCES ON GRETCHEN RUBIN'S FOUR TENDENCIES

I have many further resources to help you understand and use the Four Tendencies framework.

The main additional resource is the Better app, discussed on page 254. The Better app allows you to use the Four Tendencies to make your life *better,* by harnessing the Four Tendencies to meet your aims (or to help other people to do so); the Better app also makes it easy to form and join accountability groups.

I've created two summary guides to act as quick references to the Four Tendencies. To get a PDF, go to gretchen rubin.com to download it or to email me a request:

- The Flash Evaluation—to help you determine someone's Tendency quickly and casually

- The Nutshell Guide to the Four Tendencies—a summary of the Four Tendencies, with their strengths, weaknesses, and patterns of behavior

You can also email me to request:

- The Discussion Guide for *The Four Tendencies*—for book groups, work groups, faith- and spirituality-based groups, workshops, accountability groups, and the like

- The Starter Kit for launching an accountability group

- Further Reading on Other Personality Frameworks—if you love a good personality framework as much as I do, you'll be interested in these other works

I also frequently write about the Four Tendencies on my blog, gretchenrubin.com, and my cohost and sister, Elizabeth Craft, and I often discuss the framework on our podcast, *Happier with Gretchen Rubin*. For instance, we focus on each of the Four Tendencies in episodes 35, 36, 37, and 38.

THE BETTER APP: GRETCHEN RUBIN'S FOUR TENDENCIES

With the outstanding team at Mighty Networks, I've created an app, Better. It's all about how to use the Four Tendencies to make your life . . . *better.*

Better helps you harness the Four Tendencies framework to create a better life—and it can also allow you to help and persuade other people more effectively.

I can hardly drag myself away from the conversations in the app; people's insights, experiences, and tips are fascinating.

The Better app allows you to:

- Join accountability groups tailored to your specific Tendency. Obligers, you know you need this! Accountability that's always with you, right in your pocket.

- Meet other Obligers, Questioners, Upholders, and Rebels to get support, encouragement, and ideas for navigating your Tendency—as well as navigating other people's Tendencies.

- Join discussions on topics related to the Four Tendencies, such as:

    Work and career

    Productivity

    Children and parenting

    Guiding teams, patients, or clients

    Love and relationships

    Achieving goals

    Fun with the Four Tendencies (this is where I really let myself get whimsical)

    Building habits

    Accountability

    Better health

Learn more online at www.BetterApp.us, or search for "Better Gretchen Rubin" in the app store.

NOTES

Note about emails, posts to the blog, and other personal stories: While I've changed identifying details and edited comments for clarity and length, all the illustrations come from real people.

Chapter 1: The Four Tendencies

8 To test my observations about the Four Tendencies . . . Quantitative survey conducted by Aperio Insights among nationally representative sample of U.S. adults, geographically dispersed with mix of gender, age, and household income. Four-minute online survey fielded July 18–August 2, 2016, n = 1,564.

Chapter 3: Understanding the Upholder

38 one study of Facebook status updates . . . Matt Huston, "Status Updates Don't Lie," PsychologyToday.com, July 8, 2015, https://www.psychologytoday.com/articles/201507/status-updates-don-t-lie.

Chapter 5: Understanding the Questioner

70 one survey in which 26% of doctors agreed with the statement . . . http://www.consumerreports.org/health/resources/pdf/best-buy-drugs/money-saving-guides/english/Drug ComplianceFINAL.pdf.

71 For instance, legendary entrepreneur and business leader Steve Jobs . . . Walter Isaacson, *Steve Jobs* (New York: Simon & Schuster, 2011), pp. 43, 453–56.

Chapter 7: Understanding the Obliger

113 People who enrolled in a weight-loss program with an accountability partner . . . Kelly McGonigal, *The Will-power Instinct: How Self-control Works, Why It Matters and What You Can Do to Get More of It* (New York: Avery, 2013).

113 when a group of children was trained as "change agents" . . . Nalika Gunawardena, et al., "School-based Intervention to Enable School Children to Act as Change Agents on Weight, Physical Activity and Diet of Mothers: A Cluster Randomized Controlled Trial," *International Journal of Behavioral Nutrition and Physical Activity* 13 (2016):45.

Chapter 9: Understanding the Rebel

158 a *New York Times* article about patterns of marriage, housework, and earning . . . Claire Cain Miller and Quoc Trung Bui, "Rise in Marriages of Equals Helps Fuel Divisions by Class," *New York Times*, February 27, 2016, A1.

ABOUT GRETCHEN RUBIN

Gretchen Rubin is one of the most influential writers on the linked subjects of habits, happiness, and human nature.

She's the author of many books, including the *New York Times* bestsellers, *Better Than Before* and *The Happiness Project*. A member of Oprah's SuperSoul 100, Rubin has an enormous following, in print and online; her books have sold more than 2 million copies worldwide, in more than 35 languages; and on her popular daily blog, gretchenrubin. com, she reports on her adventures in pursuit of habits and happiness.

She also has an award-winning podcast, Happier with Gretchen Rubin.

She lives in New York City with her husband and two daughters.

THE *NEW YORK TIMES* BESTSELLER

How can we make good habits and break bad ones?

Whether you want to eat more healthfully, stop checking devices, or finish a project, the invaluable ideas in *Better Than Before* will start you working on your own habits – even before you've finished the book.

'A lot of us would like a Rubin in our lives' *The Times*

'Extraordinary' Viv Groskop

'Fascinating, persuasive' *Guardian*

'A life-changer' *The Pool*